hot tips for teachers

by
Ann Salisbury Harrison
Frances Burton Spuler

A Learning Handbook™

Published by Fearon Teacher Aids
an imprint of
Frank Schaffer Publications®

Authors: Ann Salisbury Harrison, Frances Burton Spuler

Frank Schaffer Publications®

Fearon Teacher Aids is an imprint of Frank Schaffer Publications.

Printed in the United States of America. All rights reserved.
Limited Reproduction Permission: Permission to duplicate these materials is limited to the person for whom they are purchased. Reproduction for an entire school or school district is unlawful and strictly prohibited. Frank Schaffer Publications is an imprint of School Specialty Publishing. Copyright © 1983 School Specialty Publishing.

Send all inquiries to:
Frank Schaffer Publications
3195 Wilson Drive NW
Grand Rapids, Michigan 49534

Hot Tips for Teachers

ISBN: 0-8224-3700-7

4 5 6 7 8 9 10 MAL 10 09 08 07 06 05

contents

preface

Teachers have often expressed a need for help in classroom management. Over the years, we have dropped classroom management tips one at a time to student teachers, new teachers, and co-workers, but because we hadn't organized the tips, there were gaps in their learning. This book contains all the ideas we would like to share with them.

Our lighthearted approach to this serious subject is a tip in itself. You must find humor in the business of education if you are to survive. Besides, laughter is a super stress-reliever!

While some tips are aimed at a specific age group, others cover all grade levels or can be modified to suit a grade level. The tips are grouped under such categories as **audio-visual equipment, behavior problems, make-up work,** and **yelling.** The categories themselves are alphabetized for easy reference. Whenever appropriate, we have cross-referenced related categories.

We have used the pronoun *we* when relating anecdotes because, as longtime friends, we've shared, retold, and embellished these school tales so many times, we've actually forgotten to whom they happened. Be assured, the incidents did occur. Even the cartoons dispersed throughout the book illustrate our funny-but-true classroom experiences.

We hope that by consulting *Hot Tips for Teachers* regularly, you'll find teaching easier and more enjoyable.

A.S.H.
F.B.S.

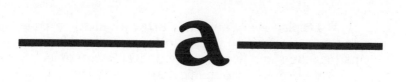

a

art

Not all children's art is perfect. Some students' drawings will make you want to giggle. Consider these rear-view drawings of cows in their stalls, sketched by a ten-year-old who was having difficulty with udder placement . . . utterly misplaced!

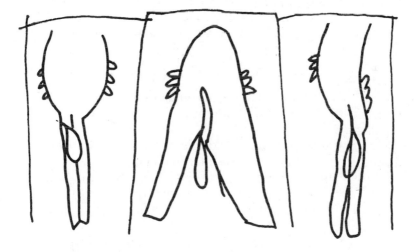

Children are serious artists and may weep at the slightest hint that you find their work less than superior. Be sure your body language and your verbal language are giving the same supportive message to the students when you're viewing their art work. (See **body language**.)

Art talent may be a student's only strength. If so, encourage the child to make the most of it. You'll both benefit.

* Display every student's art work at some time during the year. Limiting your choice to the five best means that the same five kids are chosen every time.

* Incorporate mechanical art on tests by having students color maps, draw cross sections, sketch and label, illustrate, or diagram.

* Teach lettering early in the year. Reinforce what the students learn by having them letter posters, charts, and drawings throughout the year.

* Be a thief of art ideas. Make notes as you go from class to class and from school to school. Pick your neighbor's brain for suggestions.

* Before starting an art project, ask yourself, "What is the worst thing that can happen during this project?" Then, be ready for it. If the project is too risky, nix it.

* You can prepare good art lessons from books. Do the project ahead of time yourself so you can give good directions and have a sample to show the kids.

* When you buy art supplies for your classroom, keep receipts—art supplies are tax deductible.

* Use scraps and your imagination to keep your costs down. Don't ask students to buy art supplies unnecessarily.

* Consider using old fabric, burlap, newspaper, wallpaper, or aluminum foil as a backing for your bulletin boards. These last longer, are reusable, and don't fade.

* Encourage the kids to keep art shirts at school with their names on them. You'll probably find one handy, too.

* Use water-base paints and inks whenever you can.

* When painting with students, line the floor with newspapers and work in small groups.

* Spray chalk drawings with hair spray to keep the chalk from smudging.

* If you'd like your students to work in clay but no kiln is available, add a squirt of liquid glue to each handful of clay. The glue will reduce breakage after the piece dries.

assignments

No busywork! Assignments should be challenging but not frustrating, and they should have a purpose. If an evaluator were to ask what the students were doing, make sure the students would know the objective and be able to state it. (See **objectives**.) Demonstrate the value of each assignment by correcting it, checking it, or discussing it.

* Make your rules for the use of pen or pencil on assignments clear to the students; then enforce the rules. Be prepared to deal with the question of whether or not it's all right to use erasable pens.

* Enforce your standards for headings and handwriting on every assignment.

* Inform students of deadlines and the consequences for handing work in late or not at all. Be consistent.

* Vary the methods you use for checking assignments. Kids can grade their own or switch papers with their neighbors, or you can grade them. If kids do the marking, collect the papers and check for errors in correction.

* Write personal comments whenever possible, but be sure they are constructive and positive.

* Encourage students to take papers home regularly, have their parents sign them, and return the signed papers to school for filing.

Speech bubble: I don't want to have to remind you again, Morris. You must return your report card with your parent's signature.

* Since you're accountable for what the students do, save signed papers for parent conferences.
* For related topics see **instruction**, **lesson plans**, **make-up work**, and **plan book**.

attendance

Take the time to keep your own accurate record of attendance. In some school systems, one day of inaccuracy can mean that a kid will fail a subject or a whole grade.

* A safe place to keep your own record of attendance is in your grade book.
* Write absentees' names on work sheets or tests you have prepared for the day. Store the pages in a make-up work folder and have the students complete the work when they return.
* If you ever have doubts about a parent's signature, a saved excuse note is a good way to check it.
* As you receive excuse notes for absentees, check to see that they are dated. If they are not, date

Murphy's Laws for Teachers

Students with behavior problems are never absent . . . not one day . . . all year. Make out their attendance awards in September to save time in June!

them yourself. File them in chronological order in a safe place until the office calls for them or until the last day of school.

audio-visual aids

* If your school system has a media center from which you order A-V materials, borrow the list early in the year. Then, using your textbooks, schedule what you would like to use for the year. We find that it works best to take each unit one textbook at a time and list all the A-V items related to that unit.

* Most media centers have a time limit set for prebooking, such as four weeks, six weeks, or a semester. Order a month's worth of A-V aids rather than one film or filmstrip at a time. Thinking ahead helps to keep you paced. (See pacing.)

* As you write orders for A-V materials, include the number of minutes the A-V material runs. Then, if you receive confirmation that the material is coming to you, write the name of the A-V aid, how long it is, and the chapter it belongs to in the place in your plan book for when you'll be using it. It'll jump out at you if you write it in color.

* One way to file confirmation slips is to paste them in a notebook by subject, unit, and chapter. Next to each confirmation slip, jot down possible test questions and discussion points for the chapter and ideas for correlating it with art, music, or physical education. Also paste in copies of related handouts.

* Offer to share the ordering of A-V materials with others on your grade level or in your department. This saves time. Work out an arrangement to view them together, thus saving electricity and wear and tear on the materials and equipment.

* As you use A-V material, be very critical. Do not hesitate to ax from your list any material that does not hone in on your lesson's objectives.

* A-V materials often arrive early or late. Be flexible. Use them as preparation for an upcoming lesson or as a review of a lesson already taught.

audio-visual equipment

* Never allow a student, no matter how old, to move a television. You are responsible if the child is injured while moving equipment. TV sets have toppled off carts and killed children.

* Suggest rather than assign a TV program for kids to watch. Their parents may have planned to watch a different program.

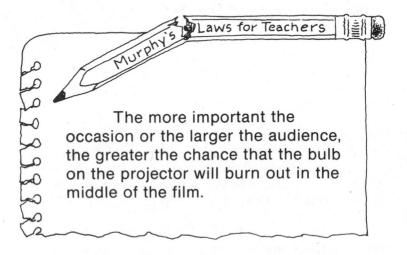

Laws for Teachers

Murphy's

The more important the occasion or the larger the audience, the greater the chance that the bulb on the projector will burn out in the middle of the film.

* If you have access to a television set at school, check the listings for educational TV programs that correlate with your lessons. Sign out the TV for the appropriate time and day. Write this in your plan book.

* Students from about grade 4 up can run A-V equipment with guidance and thorough training. Let them do it.

* If you're checking out a projector for several showings, or if your classroom is a good distance from the check-out place, sign out an extra bulb.

* For a related topic see **opaque projector.**

awards

Children (and adults) love to be awarded. You can create awards at little or no cost by making them out of scraps of construction paper or from a homemade ditto. You can order printed awards from teachers' magazines or purchase them from school supply stores.

* Make certain that every student receives an award sometime during the year. Granted you might have to search for something to award, but even an award for loud singing will convey a positive feeling to a student that will last longer than a pat on the back.

* Give awards for scholastic achievement only to those who actually deserve them. One of something means a lot, but if you and seven of your classmates receive the same award, some of the meaning is lost.

* Institute a Student of the Month award in your school. This works well in secondary schools, where many teachers have the same student.

* Avoid such awards as best dressed, prettiest, or best looking. Kids don't have a lot of control over the quality of their clothing or their physical attributes.

* Awards don't all have to be in superlatives. Give awards for a neat desk, cooperation, an interesting lunch, creativity, memorization of a long poem, being a fast paper-passer-outer, ten library books read, or a zillion more things along this line. Be imaginative!

b

bathroom

∗ Be aware of students with specific elimination problems (either permanent or temporary) by checking health records or asking for notes from home. Let the class know that you care about their physical well-being and that you want them to be comfortable in your classroom. (See **health: physical and mental.**)

∗ If a student needs to use the bathroom often, seat the student near the door to make his or her coming and going less distracting to others.

∗ Set standards for the proper use of the bathroom. When children are allowed to linger unattended in a bathroom, trouble usually results. Periodically look in on the restroom of your own sex to check on behavior.

∗ If you have a restroom in your classroom, place lines of tape about 60 cm apart outside the door to indicate where each waiting person is to stand. Some teachers place interesting work sheets or brain-teaser activities in waiting areas to prevent disruptive behavior.

beginning the day

The climate of the day starts the minute a student walks into class. Be there and be ready!

∗ Assemble all materials for the day in the order in which they will be used.

∗ Check your Daily Reminder File (see **daily reminder file**) for items to be taken care of right away. Complete all forms in today's file and send them on their way.

* Write the schedule for the day on the board. This sets the pattern for the students and eliminates a zillion questions. Also, if you forget that your library period begins at 10:37 and it is now 10:36, it's guaranteed some kid will remind you!

* Write plans for the first period of the day on the board and hang charts.

* If your class seems able to handle quiet conversation or work on games of their choice, let them improve their social skills at this time.

* If your class needs constant direction, have a board-work assignment to provide structure for the students upon their arrival at school. Board-work activities can be simple brain-teaser activities or reinforcement work from your teacher's manual. A simple list of possible activities written on the board lets the students know what is expected upon arrival:

Make-up work (priority for yesterday's absentees)
Quiet game (checkers, chess, educational games)
Silent reading or study for tests
Assignment: Drill work, Math, Set 34, Page 336

Such a list helps students to make good use of their time while allowing them to make their own choices. It also gives you time to complete necessary tasks.

beginning the year

* Bulletin boards take time to construct, so start early. Have all bulletin board items laminated, cut out, and ready to assemble. Have slogan letters cut out and put each word in a separate envelope.

* Run off dittos you know you will use, staple them in sets, and stack them in color-coded folders ready to distribute. (See **grouping**.)

* Order A-V materials and assemble the equipment you want to use on the first day.

* Scout around the school and find out where, how, and from whom to get materials for your classroom. Plan your first day and have on hand a few time fillers so you don't get caught short.

* For related topics see audio-visual aids, audio-visual equipment, beginning the day, bulletin boards, calendars, control, discipline, files, first day, pacing, schedules, and text and workbooks.

behavior problems

You've posted the rules for discipline, you have begun the year just like all the textbooks say, and you've read the manuals that your school and your school system put out. All of a sudden, you find a student in your class with trouble in the eyeballs. You can just sense it. Welcome to the wonderful world of teaching!

The tips below for handling a troublesome student are chronological. In other words, don't have a conference with a parent until you have tried a few other techniques. In our experience, you will need to go through only the first six steps most of the time. These day-to-day methods will prove to be effective in maintaining discipline in your classroom.

* *Shoot for new vibes!* While you are teaching, walk over and stand near the troublesome student. This action puts you in control of the student, who may straighten up with such a reminder.

* *Shoot for a distraction!* Call on the student to give a response to a question, to read a passage aloud, to point to a place on the map, or to do any other thing you can think up. This temporarily takes the student's mind off being troublesome and puts it on the work, where it belongs.

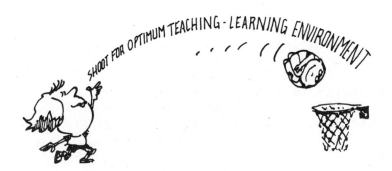

✻ *Shoot the look!* Give a troublesome student a look that would rot socks! This acknowledges that the student is acting inappropriately and that you find the behavior unacceptable. This does not disturb others.

✻ *Shoot to touch!* Walk over to a troublesome student while you are teaching and gently touch the student. When the student looks at you, shake your head or put your finger to your lips to let it be known that the behavior is still inappropriate and unacceptable.

✻ *Shoot with a word!* Give a troublesome student a one-liner, stated with authority, that requires no answer. "Cool it!" works well. You can usually catch three other students you didn't know were misbehaving.

✻ *Shoot with a statement!* Speak directly to the behavior. In your mind, separate the behavior from the child—they are not the same. Say "Your talking is distracting the class" rather than "You are distracting the class." What you want to do is eliminate the unacceptable behavior, not the kid.

✻ *Shoot for a time-out!* Physically move a troublesome kid quietly and quickly to a predesignated "time-out" spot in your classroom.

✻ *Shoot for counseling!* Speak to the troublesome child outside the classroom. You may ask a student to wait for you outside the classroom, but since you are legally responsible for the student, you should get outside as soon as possible. Use your judgment in each situation as to how long this student can safely wait for you. When you speak to the student, try not to become angry. You still want the student to stop the inappropriate behavior. Documenting begins here. Write on an index card, "Pat distracting class with talking; spoken to outside class, March 24, 1983, 10:05 A.M."

✻ *Shoot with a note!* Write a brief note to a troublesome student's parent describing the child's behavior and the methods you have tried to eliminate the behavior. Include the effects the behavior is having on the student. Document the fact that you sent a note or keep a copy of it.

✻ *Shoot with a phone call!* You want the parent to cooperate in eliminating the unacceptable behavior that the child exhibits. Realize that while the parent is probably angry at the child, the parent may displace the anger to you. Listen quietly, then ask the parent to work with you to help the child. The message you want to convey is that you care about the student. Document this phone call.

✱ *Shoot for a conference!* Arrange for a conference with a troublesome student's parent. Here again, describe the behavior and ask for the parent's help in eliminating the unacceptable behavior. Ask for suggestions and arrange to get together again to discuss improvement. Keep in mind that no matter what the reason the child or the parent gives you for the behavior, you still want it stopped. For instance, sad as it may be that the child's home life is unhappy, the student's incessant talking in class is distracting to you, to the student, and to others—it must be stopped. Your goal is to help children handle crises, not to allow them to make excuses for unacceptable behavior because there are crises. Document the conference.

✱ *Shoot yourself and the kid to the office!* Before taking the kid to the office, inform the building administrator of the steps you have taken up to this point. Again, state the unacceptable behavior and ask for suggestions.

✱ *Shoot for outside help!* Discuss what steps need to be taken with the building administrator.

✱ *Shoot for an arrangement!* For some reason, a student who is a behavior problem in your classroom may behave beautifully in someone else's classroom. While you are waiting for positive steps to be taken, arrange with a colleague to trade children who exhibit unacceptable behavior at times. It would be better that the student hear a lesson in another classroom and get something out of it than ignore the lesson in your classroom and prevent the other kids from hearing it, too.

✱ Be aware of changes in a student's behavior or appearance. Immediately notify the proper resource people of any of the following symptoms:

squinting
listlessness
overtiredness
malingering
poor attendance
inappropriate dress for the weather
severe change in handwriting
dropping grades
unexplained crying
unexplained bruises
personality changes
withdrawn manner
self-inflicted wounds

    * For related topics see **attendance, child abuse, health: physical and mental,** and **text and workbooks.**

body language

    Nonverbal communication can take positive and negative forms. Facial expressions, physical nearness or contacts, and gestures are all ways to communicate nonverbally. Your nonverbal messages speak as clearly as your verbal ones.

    * Be certain that your nonverbal messages and your verbal messages match. Children pick up on inconsistencies quite early. If you busily complete a report for the office while a child relates a story to you, the child and the rest of the children know you aren't interested. Verbally you may have said you were interested, but nonverbally—even though you nod occasionally to indicate that you are listening—you show you are not. It would be better to have the child postpone telling the story until you can listen and show interest.

    * Catch the eye of a disruptive student in the auditorium and give the student a stern look to stop the unfavorable behavior. Nonverbal discipline takes the least time and is the least disruptive of all the methods of discipline. If effective, it's the easiest. You may want to perfect a look that says "Stop it so I don't have to speak to you!"

books

(See book sets, classroom library books, professional library books, and text and workbooks.)

book sets

＊ To have books returned to their proper places in sets, line up each set of books in order, with the first volume on the left and the last volume on the right. Attach a strip of colored tape to the top of the first volume and run it diagonally down to the bottom of the last volume. Snip the tape between the books with scissors and press down the edges. Presto! You can see from across the room that if the tape runs in a diagonal line, the books are all there.

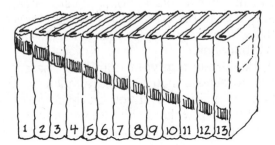

＊ Use outdated textbooks as resources or supplementary materials. If discarded textbooks are available, ask for a set for your room.

bulletin boards

＊ Use few colors, large simple objects, and one idea per bulletin board.

* Place most of the bulletin board's contents at the kids' eye level, or make the items large enough for them to see from their desks.

* Use large, easy-to-read lettering. Avoid using vertical lettering because it is difficult for many children to read.

* Have slogan letters cut out and paper-clipped together in correct order. Save the words in envelopes and write the slogan on the front of the envelope.

* To get an idea of how your bulletin board is going to look, first pin up the items for easy shuffling around before the final staple job.

* Consider using your bulletin board space to post the fixed items in your schedule, such as PE, lunch, music, art, or library. Bulletin boards displaying a calendar, speller of the month, students' classroom responsibilities, or school news can be arranged in September, and additions or deletions can be made regularly.

* Look out for ratty or outdated bulletin boards. We knew a teacher whose Thanksgiving turkey bulletin board was still around on Valentine's Day. When another teacher commented, a huge red heart appeared on the turkey!

Supplies

* Use a set of plastic pin-back letters. They are a true timesaver.

* Use plastic freezer containers or margarine tubs as storage containers for bulletin board letters.

* Corrugated bulletin board borders, available in school supply stores, make a board look neat and attractive with very little effort. They are reusable.

* Borrow a set of neat letter stencils from a veteran teacher to make your own set.

* If your school does not purchase bulletin board backing (which comes in a dozen colors on huge rolls), find it in a school supply catalog and show the item to whoever has the money and the authority to spend it. The rolls can be kept in a central location for all to use.

Backing Tips

* If your bulletin board backing is too large for the board, crease the edge with your fingernail and then slide an open scissors or razor edge in the crease for a neatly cut edge. This takes some practice, but once you have the hang of it, you'll find it saves precious time.

* Use newspaper, cloth, wallpaper, rug squares, or cork squares as a backing. Be inventive.

* For a related topic see **opaque projector.**

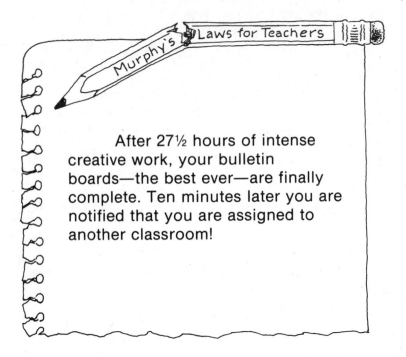

Murphy's Laws for Teachers

After 27½ hours of intense creative work, your bulletin boards—the best ever—are finally complete. Ten minutes later you are notified that you are assigned to another classroom!

C

cafeteria

* If your cafeteria is a trouble spot in your school, spend extra time reviewing the school policy in detail with your students prior to their first school lunch. Some youngsters may benefit from a practice run.

* Set your limits and your standards. Know exactly how you will get your students to the cafeteria in an orderly manner, how you will pick them up, and what students should do if they have no money and no bag lunch.

* Daily as you go to lunch, give students feedback about the good ways they are behaving. This often keeps a class on a good behavior track when you cannot be with them.

* Knowing when students need to vent excess energy and allowing them the time and space to do it often prevents misbehavior in the cafeteria. Rainy days

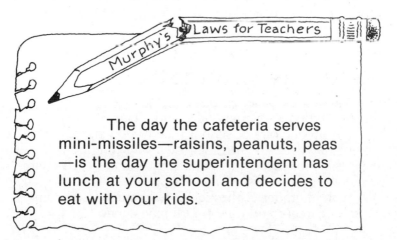

Murphy's Laws for Teachers

The day the cafeteria serves mini-missiles—raisins, peanuts, peas —is the day the superintendent has lunch at your school and decides to eat with your kids.

and limited outside activity can make a class spirited at lunch, but several rousing games during the day could help settle them down. Reading a quiet story just before going to lunch helps set the mood.

* Take strong disciplinary measures if necessary. If two kids apparently cannot sit next to one another in the lunchroom without a disturbance, separate them immediately. If the entire class seems excessively noisy, assign seats for a short period until manners are restored.

* Return to the cafeteria before the end of the lunch period to ensure an orderly dismissal.

calendars

* In an obvious spot in your classroom, post all the calendar events that pertain to the students. This saves questions.

* If you have planned a busy month for your class, send a calendar home to prepare parents for upcoming events. This is a good public relations technique: It gives the parents a chance to plan ahead or to volunteer to help out in ways you never dreamed they could, and it lets them in on the good stuff that is going on in your room or school.

* So that parents know their children *did indeed* do something in school on any particular day, send home a monthly calendar that includes the objectives of upcoming lessons.

career education

It is the obligation of every teacher to help prepare students for their life's work. This obligation begins from day one of school. The wee kindergarteners will one day need to earn their own way. We are responsible for helping those little individuals earn their way skillfully, successfully, and happily.

* In grades K through 6, help students become aware of careers and the opportunities open to

everyone. Students in this bracket need to be introduced to the personal and social significance of work. Learn about as many occupations as you can with the children and examine different kinds of lifestyles. Use books, plays, role playing, speakers, films, or bulletin boards to introduce many jobs. Help the students to recognize their own values by proposing open-ended situations, showing filmstrips and movies, and handing out values worksheets. During this period, students should begin to notice what they do well and what they like to do.

* In grades 7 and 8, students begin to explore careers. Introduce students to the "cluster concept"—jobs grouped together in a related field such as health: ambulance driver, doctor, hospital housekeeper, nurse, and anesthetist. The students continue to zero in on their interests and abilities and become more aware of their own values and needs through assessment instruments, books, and films. It is in this period that they can begin to identify careers they would like to explore. Guidance in the appropriate courses needed for careers begins in this period. For example, a student who aims for a career in engineering needs to get on the right math track at this time.

* In grades 9 and 10, a more detailed study of occupations can be started and the beginning of students' skill development may take place. Whether or not to go to college is a consideration at this time. The noncollege student must have a marketable skill, and it is the responsibility of the school to prepare the youngster with a skill. To that end, teachers can help the students know their interests and abilities and find the right job for those interests and abilities. For the noncollege-bound student, encourage courses in business, electronics, computer science, or architectural drafting. A vocational-technical school within your school system is the perfect place for students to gain saleable skills and earn credits for graduation. Courses offered may include medical transcription, legal transcription, carpentry, horticulture, welding, automobile body repair, automobile mechanics, and cosmetology, among others.

College-bound students can also benefit from the courses offered at vocational-technical schools; they, too, will need jobs during the summer or part-time work while they attend college. Students should be told about the alternatives to college, including apprenticeship programs, two-year colleges, on-the-job training, correspondence schools, and military service.

    ✱ Students in grades 11 and 12 must be prepared for a post-high school choice. Make sure that each student knows that there are many options.

    ✱ Career education is not a one shot deal. As you plan the lessons from your texts, tie in the world of work to what the kids are learning. There are many ways career education information can be incorporated into your daily lessons:

1. Post pictures of workers performing various jobs.
2. Read stories to the students about workers and their jobs.
3. Show films about workers.
4. Have younger students role-play various jobs—for example, using the symbolic hats of nurse, firefighter, and baker.
5. Invite students' parents to speak about their occupations.
6. Invite guest speakers from the community to visit the class.
7. Require book reports on occupations.
8. Suggest a specific occupation or worker as a topic for an English essay.
9. Prepare a sex-equity career bulletin board showing male and female truckdrivers, male and female doctors, and male and female secretaries.
10. Assign projects involving the making of scrapbooks, posters, displays, or dioramas about various jobs.
11. Provide self-administered, job-related interest inventories with questions pertaining to students' preferences.
12. Provide resource materials, such as government publications, brochures, books, and career magazines.
13. Prepare a poster showing the many jobs that an

interest in a particular subject can lead to. For instance, the poster headed *Math* could show branches labeled *Engineer, Actuary, Teacher, Electrician,* and *Computer Programmer.*

14. Encourage your library to develop a career education section.

15. Encourage students to volunteer their services in chosen areas; for example, students interested in nursing careers may volunteer as candy stripers, and students interested in veterinary medicine may do volunteer work at the local SPCA.

16. Encourage students to look for part-time jobs in areas of their interests. A student interested in interior design may look for a job in a furniture store. A student who has an interest in teaching may look for a job with the recreation department.

* Help students view the world of work in a more positive way by providing students with:

1. knowledge of themselves
2. knowledge of a multitude of jobs, including their advantages and disadvantages
3. ways to prepare themselves for these jobs.

* Keep stressing:

1. All work has worth.
2. The work one chooses governs one's whole lifestyle.
3. The more closely matched your career is with your interests and abilities, the happier your future should be.
4. Career education is a lifelong process.

chain of command

* Know who's who in your school and in your system. Make it your business to be able to recognize your own evaluators (principal, assistant principal, supervisors, chairpersons, and key administrative personnel).

* Know to whom you should go for help with school-related problems and in what order you should go to them.

* Know what each person will be looking for. For instance, if your math supervisor has just walked into your room and expects to see you teaching math but you have lingered just a mite over your language lesson, you'd better get hot on the math lesson. You are accountable for what your schedule said you would be doing.

chaperones

Field Trips

* Be selective in your choice of chaperones. There are children who, because of a sèvere health problem or a serious discipline problem, warrant the presence of a responsible, assertive parent on a class trip.

* At the beginning of the year, ask for volunteers who would be willing to serve as chaperones. Encourage fathers as well as mothers to volunteer. In addition, let it be known that volunteers from the entire community would be welcome.

* If you have difficulty finding or selecting chaperones, consult the teacher who had your class the previous year for possible candidates.

School Dances

* If you are asked to be a chaperone:

1. Be alert for problem areas. Hallways, stairways, and bathrooms need special attention.
2. Move about often.
3. Arrive early and never, ever leave until the last student has gone.
4. Remember to check areas outside as well as inside.

* If it is your job to recruit chaperones:

1. Recruit more helpers than you actually need. These helpers must be people you can depend on. They must

be willing to stay the whole time. Stagger the chaperones' hours if no one wants to stay for the entire event.

2. Hire an off-duty police officer if you need extra help.

3. Foresee the worst that could possibly happen, and plan what you would do if the worst *did* happen.

4. Make sure parents know what time the activity ends so that the students are picked up promptly.

5. Go the extra step to be cautious. If you have a group of students waiting for rides well after the activity is over, wait with them to prevent a student from walking home without written permission or to prevent a student from thumbing a ride.

* For related topics see **field trips** and **health: physical and mental**.

charts, graphs, and posters

Most systems buy textbooks to be used for perhaps five years. Each time you make something that relates to your textbook this year, you save time for the next year. You justify the extra time spent this year when you can use the item again.

* If you've put a lot of time and effort into drawing an intricate chart, graph, or poster for a lesson that is to be repeated, cover the display with clear contact paper, store it with your bulletin board stuff, and use it year after year.

* Incorporate into a bulletin board a good chart that was once used in teaching a lesson. The bulletin board then becomes a teaching aid—colorful and teacher-made.

* For a related topic see **opaque projector**.

checklists

Just one carefully written checklist can ward off thirty-seven new gray hairs. Having something concrete to read and mark allows you to think of more important stuff. There are different kinds of checklists; each one is a time saver and should keep you from the crazies!

✱ Make a temporary roster of students for the very first day. After a few days, when you are fairly certain of your class roster, alphabetize the names and make a ditto of your roster. Make columns about 3 cm wide on the ditto. Make about twenty-five copies and save the ditto master. This form will save you scads of time during the school year as you use it for:

1. a record of conferences (who's coming and who's not)
2. a record of books (who has what number)
3. a record of assignments or forms (what's been handed out and returned)
4. a record of gifts to be acknowledged
5. name draws (cut the roster into strips)
6. a master grade sheet
7. a record of progress reports sent
8. a record of fees paid

✱ If you trade classes or students, ask other teachers to make dittoed rosters of their classes. Then, give each teacher a copy of your roster so that they may post their grades on it. Do the same for their classes.

✱ Make up other kinds of checklists to record:

1. general items you must tell every parent at conferences
2. specific items you want to tell individual parents at a conference (See **conferences.**)
3. general items you must tell new students and their parents
4. parts of projects to be completed
5. skills covered in reading and math
6. names of students needing remediation
7. individual student progress
8. supplies and materials needed or issued to you
9. the opening and closing of school, with items listed in chronological order (Save the checklist from year to year, adding or deleting items as needed.)

10. classroom responsibilities at the end of each day (for example, shades pulled and windows locked)

child abuse

Child abuse and child neglect cases are probably found in *every* grade in *every* school. Look for them. You are legally bound to report any known or suspected case of child abuse or child neglect to your school principal, to the school nurse, or directly to the proper agency. You must report it or have the abused child report it. You may report this anonymously; the name of the person reporting the suspicion is, by law, kept confidential. The agency will require you to give them as much information as you can as to why you suspect child abuse or child neglect. Agencies who handle child abuse or child neglect cases help the entire family through counseling in addition to rescuing the child from an awful situation.

* If a student or parent wishes to talk with you and you sense he or she may be leading up to this topic, before the conversation begins, say that you must report any suspicion of child abuse or child neglect. Tell the student or parent you cannot keep his or her confidentiality on these subjects. While you don't want to put off the troubled parent or child, you must be honest. An acceptable thing to say is, "What you say to me is confidential. However, the law says that I must report any suspicion of child abuse or child neglect."

* *As soon as you have suspicions, report them.* The agency has experience in investigating this type of problem and can decide if it is in fact a child abuse or child neglect case.

* Signs that may indicate that a child has been abused or neglected are:

unexplained bruises
inappropriate dress for the weather (long sleeves in ninety-degree weather may be covering up bruises)
poor attendance

dropping grades
unexplained crying
fatigue
listlessness
withdrawn manner
overly aggressive attitude
malingering
personality changes
promiscuity
severe change in handwriting
change in work habits
self-inflicted wounds

* Ask your school in-service chairperson to consider an in-service seminar on child abuse and child neglect. The topics could include how to recognize abused or neglected children, the school's legal responsibility, the teachers' legal responsibility, the procedure for reporting child abuse or child neglect in your area, and how the local agency deals with cases of child abuse or child neglect.

classroom library books

* To enlarge your classroom library:

1. Ask students to bring in books they want to discard.
2. Order free books offered as bonuses by book clubs when your students order.
3. Use additional funds offered to you for your class to purchase books.
4. Ask friends for books that their children have outgrown.
5. Check yard sales and flea markets.
6. Ask the community or school library for their discarded books and repair them for your classroom library.
7. Offer to help retiring teachers clean out their classrooms and ask for discards.
8. Offer to help transferring teachers move—they tend to discard good junk.

* Don't run a lending library. Checking out and checking in books that belong to your classroom library really takes a lot of time. If kids want books badly enough to steal them, we'd really want them to have the books. A word or two at the beginning of the year about taking good care of your classroom library books is all that is needed.

clothes

* Display by your dress that you respect or feel good about yourself, your job, your profession, and your authority.

* Your appearance is a factor in the evaluations you receive. Know the message you want to put out.

* To avoid conflict, do not wear an item that students are prohibited from wearing.

* Wear shoes that are appropriate for the activities you have planned for the day. Think in advance, and inform your students to do likewise. A twelve-year-old girl who will be asked to run the 50-yard dash for her physical fitness test will have a difficult time if she's wearing 3-inch heels.

* Keep a sweater for cool weather and a cover-up shirt for dirty work at school.

* Bring a change of clothes for the volleyball game after school or for a cocktail date at 4:30. Some outfits are not appropriate for school.

* Take one last look in the mirror (front and back) before leaving for school. If you were a supervisor, how would you judge your appearance?

communication: nonverbal

(See body language.)

communication: oral

Effective oral communication means saying what you want to say so that the listener understands your message. The speaker and the listener can decide whether they have reached an understanding through two-way communication or through feedback.

* The first rule in oral communication is to know your audience. Do not talk down to your audience or confuse it by using educational jargon. (See jargon.) Most parents will not understand the use of terms such as *LD* or *PL-94-142* until those terms are explained. However, the parent does not want to be treated as an inferior.

* Be sensitive to other people's feelings.

* Be sincere.

* Be consistent. Set your manner and stick to it.

* Do not be afraid to say "I don't know."

* Be professional and maintain your dignity in all oral communication situations.

* Greet everyone inside and outside the classroom with a friendly hello.

* Greet all visitors warmly and sincerely. But if you do not have time to visit, say so; schedule another time that is convenient for both of you.

* Be attentive to the other person and do not interrupt.

* Set a good example for your students by saying exactly what you mean. For instance, don't just say to your class "It's twelve o'clock, boys and girls" when what you mean is "It's time to line up for lunch." Insist that your students communicate effectively with you. The child who complains of a headache could be answered with "I'm sorry." Let the child ask to be excused to go to the clinic. Have the students tell you exactly what they want. Repeated work on this can bring excellent results and make more effective communicators of children.

* Be sure you understand what the other person has said before you respond. Ask for clarification if you need it. People have different connotations for words, and messages are often unclear.

* Do not be offended if something you have said is not understood. Merely reword your statement and try to give an easily understood example.

* State everything, no matter how awful, in positive terms. For instance, instead of saying that a kid is a liar, you may say to the mother that "Lloyd needs to work on being more truthful."

* Orally encourage all students. Openly praise honest effort and take opportunities to say something nice.

* The following are some ways you may practice effective oral communication with your class:

1. Set aside time in your language arts schedule for practicing oral communication.
2. Develop a chart of ways to communicate effectively

(this works best as a combined teacher/students activity). Hang the chart in your classroom.

3. Ask questions in complete sentences and request answers in complete sentences.

4. Get a telephone and practice answering properly, taking messages correctly, and ending conversations politely.

5. Practice oral communication in small and large groups. In small groups, there are more opportunities for participation. Each person should have a chance to speak, but no interruptions should be allowed from the listeners. In large groups, students should raise their hands to be recognized. They should stand, speak clearly, and keep statements and questions brief.

6. From the start, children need chances to stand before the class and speak. Conduct oral reports, skits, role playing, puppet shows, and debates.

* For related topics see **directions** and **listening**.

communication: written

You are a teacher, and everyone expects teachers to be able to spell, punctuate, and use correct grammatical construction.

* Whenever you write anything, have a co-worker check it, if possible, or, if you rely on your own judgment, read it several times for errors.

* When checking your own work, look for:

spelling errors
punctuation errors
incorrect grammatical construction
words or sentences that may be misunderstood by
   the reader

* Word every statement in a positive manner.
Will the note you've written achieve parent cooperation,
or will you receive an angry phone call?

* Include a little humor, if it is appropriate, so
that parents know that you are human, too.

* The business of the school is to make
successes of children. Convey this in any written
communication to a parent about helping a child. You
want the parent to know that you sincerely believe the
child can overcome the problem and be a success.

* Date all notes sent and received.

* If you save a note from a parent for future
reference, write additional comments right on the letter.

* Our assignments demonstrate our ability to
communicate in writing. Do not use dittos that are
difficult to read.

* If your handwriting is poor, *type* your
messages to parents and work on your handwriting.
Cursive writing does not have to be lovely to be
effective, but it must be legible.

* Use clean stationery—not the back of your
lunchbag—to write notes.

community

* Know the socio-economic level of the
community from which your school draws.

* Before you announce a field trip for which the
kids must pay, find out if there is a monetary source to
take care of kids who can't pay.

* Let parents get to know you and make an
effort to know them. People tend to be afraid of things
that are new or unclear to them. The more they know
about what you are doing, what sort of person you are,

how you manage your classroom, how you relate to their child, and how you feel about classroom issues, the better they will feel about you and the educational experience. The following suggestions may help.

1. Ask early in the year if school patrons have any special talents that they would be willing to share with your students. Then don't hesitate to call on them.

2. Ask parents to chaperone dances, field trips, or parties.

3. Solicit parent sponsors for the Booster Club, the band, or other clubs.

4. Invite parents to participate in Career Day at school.

5. In upper grades, conduct a "shadowing" activity. This involves a student following a worker on the job for a period of time.

6. Ask parents and patrons to volunteer at athletic events.

7. Ask parents to phone other parents to set up teacher conferences.

8. Encourage parents to attend conferences, open houses, PTA meetings, schoolwide activities, or private luncheons.

   * You are accountable to every taxpayer for the monies spent on education. Don't forget citizens in the community who don't have children in the school. Ask your students to invite these citizens to school events, or notify them by letters, PTA announcements in local newspapers, or community flyers.

   * You and your school will be topics for discussion in the community. Make the discussion a pleasant and informed one by letting the parents know of the good things going on in school. (See **newspapers**.)

   * Make provisions for feedback from parents. Two-way communication is important for them. They would like to have input into their children's education. In any written communication from school, include a section for comments from the parents that may be returned to school.

   * For a related topic see **public relations**.

competition and contests

A goal of education is self-competition. One can always do better than one did before.

✱ Encourage self-competition in simple forms: Have all those who did better this week than last week on the spelling test line up first. Award simple prizes—first places in line, extra free time, the chance to choose a book to be read aloud to the class—to students who brought back their signed papers, federal cards, or book money.

✱ There will always be competition among children. Some children thrive on it and others hate it, but children need to be taught how to accept winning and losing. Encourage losers to congratulate the winners no matter how awful the losers may feel.

✱ Remind children repeatedly that playing the game is fun. Remind them from kindergarten on by asking questions such as: Who played better today than yesterday? Who had fun today? Who made it to first base or who learned a new skill? De-emphasize the win/lose aspect and emphasize the rewards inherent in playing the game: increased skill, physical activity, togetherness, fun, excitement, and a feeling of accomplishment. Also emphasize cooperation as a goal. (See cooperation.)

✱ Prior to a game or competitive activity, motivate your students to make every effort to do better than their previous best. Have them ask themselves: How were my skills? Did I hit the ball farther? Did I run as fast as I could? Did I cheer my team members on to do better? Did I spell more words correctly? Did I know more math facts? Did I cooperate with my teammates?

✱ Discuss being a good sport before every game or competitive activity. Ask questions such as "When you are on the losing team, how do you like the winners to behave?" or "When you win, how do you want the losers to behave?"

✱ Vary activities from day to day to promote different types of skills. Activities could include running games, passing or throwing ball games, eye-hand coordination games, gymnastics, multiplication facts relay, and science facts drills. Give every child an opportunity for success.

✱ Our society is heading toward more leisure time and longer life spans, both of which will give today's kids a lot of nonworking time. Help them find constructive ways to spend the time. Introduce the concept of individual sports—archery, tennis, swimming, bowling, racquetball—as opposed to team sports—soccer, football, baseball, lacrosse.

✱ Make competitive teams as equal in ability as you possibly can. If it seems that all the brighter students in your class are in row 5 or all the best kickers are on team 1, either separate them or compete another way. Make the change ahead of time, however, not in the middle of the game.

conferences

While we welcome visitors to the room, some times are inappropriate. If someone comes at an inconvenient time, offer an alternate time or offer to phone the parent later to settle on a convenient time. Some guidelines for conferences are:

* Make clear the purposes for a conference. Conferences have three purposes: information getting, information giving, and problem solving.

* Prepare for conferences with papers, notes, reports, and your grade book.

* If a parent phones the office and schedules a conference for which you can think of no cause, prepare anyway. Be pleasantly surprised if the parent simply drops off the old books that were promised you for your classroom library or brings handmade holiday wreaths.

* If you are the least bit suspicious that a parent's anger may get out of hand during the conference, schedule the parent conference in the office and ask the assistant principal or the principal to sit in.

* When you are scheduling parent conferences, first call those who most need a conference so that they may have the widest range of times to choose from. You *want* them to come.

* Have a checklist ready for all the conference items you want to mention:

attendance
clinic visits
general health
general appearance
peer relationships
forgotten lunch money
signed papers and notes
missed assignments
lack of supplies
grades
citizenship
organizational skills
study skills
physical education skills
strengths and weaknesses

* Do not sit behind your desk and have the parent sit in a squat, little 1st-grader chair. This immediately puts the parent in a mood of discomfort. Have an attractive place arranged for the conference. Even if it means that you both have to sit in squat, little

1st-grader chairs, you should be seated on an equal basis.

* You and the parent may mutually decide if the child should be present at the conference.

* Do not assume that a woman or a man who attends the conference is the child's parent. The person could be a stepparent, a grandparent, or a boyfriend or girlfriend. Also, be aware of interracial marriages and the progeny thereof. Ask the person what his or her relationship is to the student, thereby avoiding any chance of embarrassment or anger.

* If a parent is feeling the need to talk or to blow off steam, sit quietly and let the parent speak freely. Do not interrupt and do not take everything you hear personally.

* Establish a positive rapport for the conference. Make the first thing you say a positive statement about the student. (You may have to dig deep.)

* First ask parents what their perception of their child's problem is. Then offer what *you* think is the problem, and let them know that you need to have their help to solve the problem you have both identified.

* Let the parent know from the start that you believe there is a solution to the problem and that cooperation is necessary to solve it. State everything in a positive manner and inform parents by nonverbal as well as verbal means that you will never give up on the kid. (See **body language**.)

* Try to get a realistic picture of the home situation before you make a suggestion.

* Do not allow the parent to berate you and, for heaven's sake, do not resort to tears. If a parent becomes verbally abusive, simply say that you feel that this is not a good time for the conference and you would like to reschedule it at a time that will prove to be more beneficial for the child.

* During a conference, do not (1) compare a student with a sister, brother, or neighbor, (2) refer to another kid in the class by name, (3) negatively refer to the whole class, or (4) offer outside services that you are not able to provide personally.

36 *Hot Tips for Teachers . . . C*

* Try to make every conference end on a happy note. But if you can't and the parent leaves swearing to call the school board, inform your principal immediately. As building administrator, he or she needs to be prepared.

* Stick to the schedule on conference day. When you feel that everything that needs to be said has been said, simply rise and thank the parent for coming. The parent will rise in turn and you can escort the person to the door. This is especially necessary if you have another conference scheduled at that minute.

* Make a brief evaluation of the conference to keep for future reference. This is known disparagingly as "covering yourself," but it makes sense. Someday, if you must report what transpired between you and Mr. or Mrs. Smith, you can whip out your evaluation sheet.

* If you say at the conference that you will do anything or call anyone, make a note of it and do it promptly. This establishes credibility on your part and assures the parent that you care about the child.

confidentiality

* Apply the rule of *need to know.* Before you make a statement about a particular kid or a particular situation, ask yourself, "Who here has the need to know?" Reserve any confidential statement you must make for a private conversation with a person who has the need to know.

* Be especially careful about lounge conversation. Schools abound with volunteers, aides, helpers, part-time monitors, and substitutes, some of whom may be parents in the community. Because they work in the school, they have a right to use the lounge. If you need to blow off steam or to confide, know your audience. Place yourself in the shoes of the parents who find out that a teacher has referred to their child as a smart aleck or worse.

* Information received in a conference goes no further than the room, generally speaking. You must

decide if there is anyone else who deals with the student professionally and needs to know the information you received in the conference. If so, get the parent's permission to divulge the information. The exception is that all known or suspected cases of child abuse or incest must be reported by law. (See **child abuse**.)

✱ Do not let what a parent tells you about another teacher go any further than the room. An exception to this rule would be if there was suspicion of a child's safety being threatened by the teacher in question. Use your judgment.

✱ If you would like to read a child's written work aloud in class, ask the child's permission. When students prefer not to have their work read aloud, respect their wish for privacy.

✱ What you read in the cumulative folder is confidential to everyone except the parent, the student, or another person directly involved with the student, such as a teacher, principal, or guidance counselor.

control

The atmosphere in the classroom depends largely on who's in control. You have control, they have control, or you'll spend the year fighting each other for control. For an atmosphere conducive to learning, *you* need to be in control.

Every teacher we have known who had discipline problems lost control early in the year. If you have no control, you cannot teach. But before you can take control, you must know what you will and won't tolerate in the classroom. Knowing what you want will help you to be consistent and will give the students the structure they need.

The ultimate goal is student self-control. If you're absent or if you're called to the office, the students should be able to control themselves. You and they can achieve this by working together.

✱ Create a warm, friendly atmosphere—the

optimum condition for learning. Firmness does not negate a warm, friendly atmosphere. A low, controlled, but loving voice is all the ammo you need for most classroom situations.

    * Set your limits right at the first and be prepared to enforce them all year, because students will test you from time to time.

    * For related topics see behavior problems, lining up, responsibilities, and text and workbooks.

cooperation

    * Set up situations in your classroom that allow students to experience cooperation as well as competition. (See competition and contests.) Such situations include opportunities for students to:

1. individually set goals for what they plan to do in the group.
2. set group goals.
3. have free and open interaction among the members of the group with brainstorming sessions.
4. allow for leadership.
5. listen attentively to others' suggestions and offer their own suggestions without interruption in a give-and-take situation. (See listening.)
6. work through disagreements.
7. have the group capitalize on individual members' strengths.

    * In evaluating group projects, be sure to place emphasis on how a group functioned and not on the final product. Did the group utilize its individual members' strengths? Assign a group grade, possibly in two parts—one for the process and one for the final product.

    * Allow the group to evaluate itself both on how the members functioned as a group and on the final product.

creative writing

Good writing rarely comes out of one sitting. A daily writing time is not a bad idea. Children may use this time to correct something or to write something new.

 * Give students ample opportunities to write creatively.

 * Don't mark a child's rough draft until you have commented positively. Nothing turns off a child so quickly as red pencil marks all over the page.

 * If the work is to be displayed or published, help the child to correct it and to copy it with all the corrections. Tell the students that you want them to be as proud of their work as they can be. Remind them that they need to do their work well in order to feel this pride.

cumulative folders

You are legally responsible for the students while they are in your care. You can be sued if you are found to be negligent in your duties as their surrogate parent. Your duties include knowing pertinent student information found in the students' cumulative folders.

 * Prior to the opening day of school, go through your cumulative folders and look for health problems, such as allergy to bee stings, kidney dysfunction, vision problems, hearing problems, asthma, diabetes, or heart murmurs.

 * If there is a place for you to sign and date the viewing of a folder, do so. You may be questioned at a later date about viewing the folders, and it is a good idea to have a written record. This tip is especially true for departmentalized teachers.

 * Enter in the folder any new situation that arises while you are in charge of a child, such as new children in the family, change in parents' marital status, or special directions concerning the child.

* Keep student data up to date. Phone numbers in particular may change frequently.

* Eliminate outdated information, such as old progress reports and report cards.

* Arrange the items in each cumulative file in a specific order so that you can easily find what you're looking for.

* Know your school's regulations pertaining to viewing cumulative records.

* Keep in mind that testing information found in cumulative folders is not gospel. A test score is only one indicator of the child's academic potential, and it may be an inaccurate indicator. The kid may have been recovering from the flu on the day the test was given, or a beloved pet may have just died.

* If a student's grades from previous years have been As or Bs, but Cs and Ds are showing up this year:

1. Look for the cause.
2. Look for ways the child can improve.
3. Be prepared to justify your grades with representative samples of the child's work.
4. Inform the parents immediately.

—d—

daily reminder file

We have a method for keeping up with due dates and keeping track of the endless one-sheet forms that need to be filled out. Using file folders numbered 1 through 31 (one for each day of the month) and twelve separators (one for each month), file all the forms that come to you to be filled out. File each form in the folder for *the day before* it is due. Each morning, pull out the folder for that day. In other words, a sheet that must be returned on the 17th of the month should be filed in folder number 16. On the 16th, you'll pull out the folder, complete the form and send it on its way. Then place the empty folder at the back of the stack, behind numbers 1 through 15, which are already behind next month's separator. (See the illustration.)

A System for Keeping Up with Due Dates

While we keep our Daily Reminder File folders in a file cabinet drawer, any sturdy box 12 inches wide will do. File items daily and you'll keep up with your specified due dates. Better still, you won't spend seventeen hours looking for the one sheet you misplaced, which was due today.

directions

The purpose of giving directions is to achieve a specific outcome. If the specific outcome is not achieved, you may want to review the following tips for giving directions.

* Be totally familiar with the project before you give directions to someone else.

* Have a sample of the item in each stage.

* Have all materials assembled and ready in the order that they are needed in the project or lesson.

* Think about who is likely to have a difficult time with the project or lesson; situate this student next to a kid who'll be a whizbang at it.

* Use visual aids whenever appropriate: draw on the chalkboard, list the steps on the chalkboard, show a picture of the finished item, do the project with your students, and show each step.

* If at all possible, go through all the steps of a project orally and visually with the class before you begin step 1. This lets the students see and hear where they are headed. It also allows the whizkid the opportunity of forging ahead; then this student can help others. Do not be at all surprised if the kids who are well below average academically are super with their hands. Help them to enjoy their success by enjoying it with them.

* It is better to slow down your directions, have everyone complete the project, and be satisfied with the results than to speed through and have only one finished project—yours. Take two class periods if you must.

* Be able to give a common-sense reason for any direction. If there is no reason, nix it and let the students be creative.

* Rather than reverse all directions because you are facing the class, take a chance. Turn around and do the project over your head. Ya gotta have trust!

* If you find that your directions are unclear, do not be afraid to change them. You are not perfect.

* Be careful of how you word directions. Children tend to take directions literally.

* For a related topic see communication: oral.

discipline

* If you post rules, make them positive:

Walk in Halls
Sharpen Pencils Before Class
Enter and Leave the Room Quietly

* If two kids are fighting over ownership of an object, take the item from them and ask them both to bring notes from home stating that the object belongs to them. We have never received two notes. Give the object to the kid who brings the note.

* Don't allow kids to sit too close to one another. Proximity can increase problems.

* Give simple incentives to positive behavior: The row that quiets down first goes to lunch first. Give rather than take away. The positive approach to behavior works longer, better, and more often, with more people, than the negative approach.

* For related topics see behavior problems and control.

dress code

* Enforce the dress code, even if you don't agree with it. If you feel the dress code is too lenient or too strict, abide by it but get moving to change it.

* If students are prohibited from wearing an item, avoid conflict by not wearing it yourself.

* If the school is setting up a dress code committee, request that the committee include teachers, parents, administrators, *and* students. In our experience, having student input is a hedge against flak about unpopular rules.

duty or committee assignments

* Since you are probably going to be assigned to a committee or work group or be given a duty at your school, think ahead. Choose *your* area of interest, not theirs. Pick in advance what you want to do and ask to be assigned to it. If you must do bulletin boards in the cafeteria twice a year, volunteer for December and February, which are cinchy months to plan for.

* If you feel that a duty assignment is unnecessary or that a new one is needed, talk to the building administrator. If your school has had a field day for years, with you as the chairperson, and this year everyone sounds bored with the idea, ask the building administrator if some revisions to the old plan may be made. The two of you may come up with a better idea. However, be prepared to accept a new challenge if a new idea does arise.

* If assigned a particularly difficult job, such as planning in-service days for your school:

1. Talk to the teacher who had it last year and pick the teacher's brain.
2. Do a little research on the topic. Find out what is new, fun, or interesting.
3. Add your own ideas to give a fresh light to the topic.
4. Make whatever you plan meaningful and beneficial to all those involved.

* There are two ways to look at duty assignments or extra assignments:

1. You can choose one you have done before because you already have it organized and most of the groundwork has been done.
2. You can choose a new one because it will provide a challenge and may prevent boredom. (Boredom is a major factor that teachers feel leads to burnout.)

e

emergencies (accidents, fire drills, kidnaps, runaways)

* Remember the students' safety is first and foremost at all times.

* Mentally plan what you would do *if*. This may sound like worrying before the fact. We see it as being covered. Knowing what you would do *if* helps you avoid confusion and save precious time.

* Teach kids the procedure for evacuation from any point in the school. Students away from the class need to know where to go and, if necessary, how to get back to you.

* Before the first fire drill of the school year, have students line up in alphabetical order. Have them memorize who stands immediately before and immediately after them in line. Then, when the fire bell is

Allison Byron Chris Gallagher John at band, Lawton

sounded, have students line up randomly and file outside quietly and quickly, as they have already been directed to do. Once they are safely outside, ask them to quietly arrange themselves in alphabetical order. If you have your grade book, you can call the roll; if you don't have your grade book, the students can sound off their names, point out missing students, and account for their classmates.

  * Prepare your students for emergencies by posting rules in the room. Also, set standards for behavior during emergencies and impose them.

  * Keep your grade book or class roster handy for emergencies.

  * After taking care of a sick or injured child, find out whom you must tell or what form you must file and where.

  * If a child runs away from your classroom, notify an administrator immediately.

  * If a student confides in you that he or she wants to run away, try to talk him or her out of it *and* notify an administrator. When it's a choice between the child's safety and keeping a confidence, the child's safety comes first.

  * If you overhear that a child wants to run away, talk to the student and notify an administrator.

  * Suicides do occur among students. Notify an administrator immediately if a student threatens suicide.

  * Be aware that kidnappings from schools do occur. With the increasing number of divorces, the possibility of kidnapping (the child being taken by the noncustodial parent who has no legal right to do so) is also increasing. Know which of your students are children of divorce, who has custody, and what the restrictions are. See that the office has this information. You may have to request a copy of the court order for the child's cumulative folder.

  * To be on the safe side, never release a child from your room to an unauthorized person. Request that the person sign the student out from the office.

  * If you're getting strange vibes about a situation, don't hesitate to ask your building

administrator to check further. The child's safety is your primary concern.

* For a related topic see **safety.**

evaluation: student

(See grades, report cards, and tests and quizzes.)

evaluation: teacher

* Be aware that you are constantly being evaluated by administrators, students, parents, other teachers, and supervisors. Your reputation as a teacher is on-going, not static. Your attitude, ability to get along with others, willingness to work, expertise in the academic areas, and effectiveness in classroom management, even your appearance, are open to inspection every day, all day. This sounds awesome, but if you're conscious of the fact that you are always being evaluated, you will be more likely to make the right decisions in a given situation. Being aware helps you to put out the message you want people to get. Know your strengths and make them known to others.

* Evaluation includes things you probably would not ever think about. Be aware of the effect physical affection may have on a student and be ready to accept responsibility for your actions. This is a special caution from two teachers who really believe in hugging, touching, and loving, especially in a society that can be cold and uncaring. It sounds awfully cynical to say that a teacher shouldn't hug a kid, but our advice is that you'd better know the kid, the situation, and the possible consequences of the hug if you do choose to hug a kid. In the early grades, students may not feel anything about a hug other than that you are proud of them for their improvement in making the letter x. An older student may feel an emotional closeness and sexual stirring that will prove difficult to deal with later on.

* Know *every* one of your supervisors on sight and by name. Know how they can help you. The purpose of supervision is to improve education. However, most contact with supervisors will be for the purpose of evaluation. Let the supervisors make the first move when they arrive at the classroom door. If the supervisors are there just to make a routine call and to say hello, they'll do just that and move along. If they are there to evaluate your lesson, continue teaching and do not acknowledge their presence.

* For real insight, ask your students to evaluate you. Here are some questions we have used:

1. Is the teacher interested in the student as a person?
2. Does the teacher encourage students?
3. Does the teacher have a good reason for disciplining some students?
4. Does the teacher give the proper kind of punishment for the offense?
5. Does the teacher punish all the students the same way for the same wrong?
6. Does the teacher treat all students alike and have no favorites or pets?
7. Does the teacher maintain control?
8. Does the teacher enjoy teaching?
9. Does the teacher know the subject being taught?
10. Does the teacher stick to the subject?
11. Does the teacher explain the subject to the students and try to help the students?
12. Does the teacher use modern teaching methods?
13. Does the teacher make the subject interesting?
14. Does the teacher use films, filmstrips, tapes, and records?
15. Does the teacher keep the room neat?
16. Does the teacher have a good sense of humor?
17. Does the teacher show respect for students by not talking behind their backs to others?
18. Is the teacher friendly?
19. Is the teacher understanding?
20. Is the teacher patient with students?
21. Is the teacher clean and neat in appearance?

22. Is the teacher picky?
23. Does the teacher speak clearly?
24. Does the teacher write clearly?
25. Does the teacher have any irritating habits? If so, what are they? _____
26. What are some ways the teacher can improve? _____
_____

When we did this, students had the option of not signing the paper.

* For a related topic see clothes.

exercise and games

* Jogging, walking, playing tennis or racquetball, and just plain exercising with the health expert on television are all stress reducers. Consider asking a fellow teacher to jog with you around the football field after school. (Don't forget your running shoes.)

* Exercise with your students on the days you go out for PE with them.

* High schools have tennis courts. They are usually free. Get a little friendly competition going among staff and students.

* Find other interested teachers to form a league for volleyball games, baseball games, or tag football games.

* Try instituting annual faculty-student games of some sort.

* For a related topic see stress.

field trips

The written objectives for a field trip may be in the realm of learning experiences for the students; but deep in your heart, *your* number-one objective for the field trip is self-survival! Your number-two objective is to return to school with the same number of students you started out with, preferably in the same physical condition they left in—or better!

* Be selective about field trips, because money and fuel may be tight. Look for a possible walking trip near your school.

* Be sure to motivate the children for the trip and evaluate the trip when you've returned to class.

* Tell everyone who needs to know that you and your class will not be at school. It is courteous to inform the speech teacher that David and Anna will not be at their lesson on Tuesday.

* Know what to do *if* (See **emergencies**).

* Have each child's parents' phone numbers for that day with you. If a parent is going to be at work from 9:00 until 11:00 A.M. and will have lunch with a friend from 11:00 A.M. until 1:00 P.M., have those numbers. Leave a copy of the numbers at school.

* Consider making a seating plan for the bus. If you do this, make a copy for the principal to keep in the office.

* If you have an overly active child in your class, ask the child's mother or father to join you as a chaperone on the trip. Assign that student to his or her parent's tour group.

* Provide all chaperones with a list of the children in their group. Include the health information they may need and the emergency numbers for each child for that day.

* Consider using a dittoed roster for the information you give to the chaperones and principal.

* Have every minute of the day planned and inform your students of the agenda.

* Give the school administrator the following:

1. signed and dated permission slips
2. a copy of your list of phone numbers
3. a list of chaperones
4. the name of the bus company, the number of the bus, and the driver's name
5. a copy of the assigned seating plan
6. a list of students' names by partners and groups, with names of chaperones
7. an itinerary of your trip
8. a list of the objectives of the trip
9. a list of the safety precautions you've discussed with the students
10. a box of epsom salts for your tired feet to be used immediately upon your return

* Allow children to carry no more than they themselves can look after. (You cannot be responsible for twenty-five cameras.)

* If you plan to brown-bag it for lunch, discuss foods that travel well beforehand.

* Count students regularly and often while on the trip. Occasionally have them line up in alphabetical order so you can check. This takes about two minutes and sets your mind at ease. If you misplace a kid, being poor at math is no excuse and will not hold up in court!

* If your school has sold T-shirts and practically every kid has one, ask them to wear their T-shirts on the day of the field trip. Wearing the same color shirt could help you to identify your group. This is especially helpful in crowds.

* For related topics see **chaperones** and **transportation**.

files

* There are three ways to reuse file folders:

1. Turn them inside out.
2. Paste on new tabs.
3. Write in pencil and erase.

   * If you keep materials that have been run off for future use in your file cabinet, use color-coded folders. Put similar kinds of materials in same-color folders.

   * When a paper lands on your desk, handle it then and send it on its way. This saves you time in the long run. If you are unable to complete the work then, put it in your Daily Reminder File. (See daily reminder file.)

   * Keep files up to date and neat. Students love to file things for you; if the material to be filed is not confidential, have a competent student file it for you. This is good training in alphabetical order.

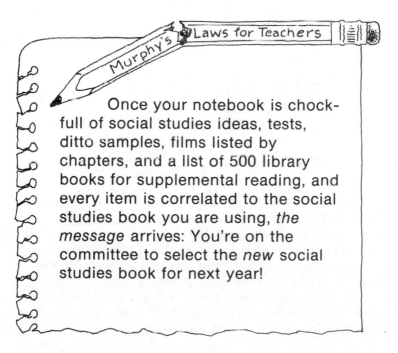

Murphy's Laws for Teachers

Once your notebook is chock-full of social studies ideas, tests, ditto samples, films listed by chapters, and a list of 500 library books for supplemental reading, and every item is correlated to the social studies book you are using, *the message* arrives: You're on the committee to select the *new* social studies book for next year!

* For documentation purposes, keep a file box on your desk with each child's name on a card. Jotting down ideas or notes concerning students is easier when the box is handy.

* Use notebooks to keep track of art ideas, suggestions for a substitute to use in class, or special plans for a subject. We tear out ideas that appeal to us from magazines or duplicate them from idea books, then paste them into the appropriate notebooks. We've kept our notebooks for years, added to them, and passed them around to dozens of colleagues, student teachers, and new teachers.

* If you are in charge of an activity, keep a notebook of how you organize the activity, dittos you use, permission slips needed, lists to check, and evaluation sheets.

* Consider having children paste in the ideas after you have selected them.

films

(See audio-visual aids.)

fire drills

(See emergencies.)

first day

* Have all materials that will go home with the students on the first day ready in stacks to hand out. Have a filled stapler ready to staple papers together or, if you are super-organized, hand them out desk by desk and staple them together before the kids even arrive.

* Post your schedule in chart form on a bulletin board or write it on the chalkboard.

* Be sure your name is written clearly on the board. Your name and a copy of the student roster should be posted on the wall just outside your door.

* Have a sample of the way you want papers headed. Either write it on the chalkboard or display it in poster form.

* Make a checklist of the topics you want to cover in the order in which you want to cover them. Consider this as a possible checklist:

1. Attendance.
2. Extra students—where do they belong?
3. No shows—ask others about these students; they might still be vacationing.
4. Assigned seats—is everyone in the right place?
5. Desks—are there enough? If not, requisition early.
6. Lunch money or bags—take care of this before lunch.
7. Bus numbers—you need to know this early enough to take care of children who were brought to school by a parent but are taking the bus home.
8. Book check—note condition and obtain acceptance signatures if using rented books.
9. Discuss standards for taking care of books.
10. Pass out and explain student handbook or school policies memorandum.
11. Pass out ditto sheet listing needed supplies.
12. Fire drill practice.
13. Discuss classroom duties.
14. Discuss lunchroom procedure.
15. Discuss procedure for lining up.
16. Discuss policies for making up work.
17. Discuss standards for heading papers and for use of pencil or ink.
18. Puzzle, word search, or game—assign if you need a few minutes of time to complete administrative tasks.

* Stand at the door when the students arrive. Your classroom management begins at that moment. Be firm, consistent, and controlled.

* As you greet the students, have something for them to do: "Good morning, Donna. It's nice to see you. Find your desk and your books and you may begin looking through them until the bell rings."

* Introduce yourself to the class.

forms

   ✱ If possible, fill out and dispatch forms in one sitting. Try to handle everything you receive then and there. If you can fill it in but can't deliver it, file it in your Daily Reminder File for the day it is due. (See **daily reminder file**.)

   ✱ When you need a form, take four: one for a goof-up, one for the next time you need one and don't have time to run to the office, one to give to a kid as a sample to take to the office if you need ten more, and one for your files. At the end of the year, return all unused forms to the proper drawers in the office.

   ✱ Use the legal name of a kid—or both the legal name and nickname—on every form. "Buster Jones" just doesn't make it.

   ✱ Even when it's not specifically requested, put your name, your room number, the date, and the grade or the subject on forms.

g

gifts

While procedures vary from school to school and from system to system, here are a few tips for those teachers whose classes exchange gifts at holiday time.

* Suggest that students donate money to a worthy cause rather than spend it on their classmates or on you.

* Suggest that students donate money to a fund and match that amount (or put in as much as you can afford) to buy games or puzzles to keep in class for free time. In upper grades, this process could involve a planning committee that checks prices around town for the best buy, presents the selections to their classmates for approval, and purchases the games and puzzles.

Of all the perfume in the world, I hate Evening in East Wauhunga worst of all.

Oh thank you, another bottle of Evening in East Wauhunga!

* If you intend to buy a gift for every member of your class, see if other teachers want to order with you to get a discount rate for bulk orders. Order early and order extra for students admitted late.

* The same tip goes for a gift fo your room parent. You might find a local merchant who'll give you a good deal if you order ten or more of an item.

* Record all gifts and thank each kid personally, using the student's name. While mailing a thank-you note to every student is expensive, students like receiving a personal thank-you note from a teacher.

* Consider sending class notes and drawings to a child who will be out for several days.

* Consider sending a sick child a free book from ones you earned by ordering for your class. Have each class member autograph it.

* Consider saving all the free books you earn until you have enough for holiday gifts to your students.

* Go in on group gifts for faculty or administrators, if possible. It's cheaper.

* If children insist on giving you a gift, take pity on their parents, who may be financially strapped at this time. If the kid asks what you'd like, say you'd really love pencils, erasers, colored markers, or note paper. You *will* love these things before the end of your first year.

* Remember janitors, maids, and cafeteria workers with jars of candy, handkerchiefs, or just the first roses of the season. Gestures like these make school a little friendlier.

goals

If you are ever asked to write out educational goals and objectives, there is an easy way to differentiate between the two:

1. *Objectives* are measurable—for example, the student will write from memory the times tables through 5s by October 15 with 80 percent accuracy. Objectives include

who does it, how, the conditions, the time frame, and *the percentage of mastery.*

2. *Goals* are immeasurable and are usually worded in terms such as *knows, learns, appreciates,* or *enjoys.* Goals are what objectives lead to.

 ✱ Objectives written in your plan book can be greatly abbreviated. Use symbols such as "/ū/" instead of writing out "The objective is to identify the long u vowel sound." Use "II" instead of writing out "Group Two."

 ✱ Since you are accountable, know what your goals for your students are. It is even better if the students themselves know what their goals are. Goals are often questioned by the students in the form of "Why do I need to learn this?" Your answer can be as simple as "The goal of this lesson is to enable you to be more well-rounded, more knowledgeable, or more aware of the world around you." Inform the students what the objective is for each lesson.

 ✱ Just before the class leaves for the day, review the goals and objectives that were covered during the day.

 ✱ Set personal goals. For example, your goal for the year may be to be more creative in your teaching. Your objectives could be to establish your art-ideas file, to use two new ideas every week, and to set aside daily a creative writing time for yourself and for your students.

 ✱ For related topics see **lesson plans** and **objectives.**

grades

 ✱ Post the letter/numerical grade equivalencies in your classroom, write them in your plan book and your grade book, and send them home with your students at the beginning of the year.

 ✱ Set up your grade book so that anyone can read it. Each entry should include what the grade is for and the date. If you have to account for what was taught and when it was taught, this record will help you.

* Set up a system of grading that is consistent for every subject you teach. If you put just a check, a check-plus, or a check-minus for homework, do this for all subjects. If you put test grades in red ink, do this for all subjects.

* For ease in averaging grades, put all numerical grades together rather than interspersing them with checks or letter grades.

* Strive for one grade per subject per week in a grading period.

* Allow students to grade their own work occasionally, but ask them to grade in pen if they have written the work in pencil. Be sure to collect the work after they grade it to check over the types of errors made.

* Report to the parent a failing grade that may appear on a report card as soon as you suspect the likelihood of such an occurrence. Give the kids as much time as possible to get back on track. Also do this as soon as you suspect there may be a drop in grades *above* failing. The parent whose *A* student receives a *C* is as upset as the parent of the *D* student who fails. Students and parents need to be aware of grades. A drop in grades may indicate a problem in the child's life that is interfering with the student's learning. Choose a progress report form, a note, a phone call, or a conference to notify parents of their child's drop in progress.

* For related topics see **report cards** and **tests and quizzes**.

greeting cards

* Save all kinds of greeting cards you receive for the pictures on them. Remove all personal messages from the inside before bringing the cards to class, unless you want your personal business read aloud by your kids.

* If you are sending a greeting card to each child, and have the time, make your own out of scraps of cloth and construction paper.

* Encourage your students to remember administrators and workers around the school at holiday time. For many reasons, cards from kids have a very special feeling attached to them.

* If your students make a card to go home, check for misspellings, but otherwise let them be as creative as they like.

* If a student is sick, ask the class or a committee to create a group card. Here again, check spelling, but allow creativity.

grouping

* Do not waste time trying to disguise the ability level of students by naming different groups. Students can figure out their own ability level in relation to the rest of the class in about 3½ minutes. So, unless you want to give groups a chance to choose jazzy names or you want to further distinguish them, don't give them names other than "Level 4" or "Level 5."

* Set your standards early in the year for behavior in the class while you are working with a group. During the first week of school, in a class group, set standards for working in smaller groups. Discuss handling distractions, working with partners, being aware of noise levels, minimizing interruptions, avoiding wasting time, completing and submitting work, and keeping busy when an assignment is completed.

* To lessen confusion, plan your groups so that you can move to them rather than having them move to you.

* Position yourself so you can observe the whole class at all times no matter what groups you are teaching.

* We've tried the rule *three before me,* and it works. Simply request that students ask their questions of three other group members before coming to you.

✱ To facilitate working with groups, color-code directions on the board with colored folders for dittoed materials. For instance, Group 1's reading text is yellow. Keep their dittoed materials in yellow construction-paper folders. Write their assignments in yellow chalk on the board. If you make charts for their group, use yellow poster board. Group 2 may be reading a blue book and Group 3's may be green. Do the same color-coordination for their groups. Buy inexpensive colored chalk at a grocery store.

✱ Plan ahead. If the same ditto will be used for three reading groups that year, run all you will need at the same time; or, better still, have the children refer to the ditto but write on other paper. In June, store the ditto for the next year.

✱ Make all visual aids to last; you'll be more inclined to use them with every group if they are made well.

✱ If you exchange classes, do not allow students to return to their homeroom for forgotten materials. Be firm. This teaches responsibility right from the start. Additionally, it is discourteous to other teachers when students disrupt lessons by wandering in to rummage through desks for forgotten assignments.

guest speakers

✱ Let your students brainstorm for whom they would like as guest speakers: industrial or manual workers, professional people, the nurse in the building—anyone with expertise in a given area of your class's interest.

✱ If your class is upper-elementary age or older, consider allowing the students to do all the work of securing the speaker, arranging the time and place, meeting the speaker on the appointed day, introducing the speaker to the audience, and arranging for any materials the speaker may need. This is great training for the students.

* Make sure you know how much time will be required for the speaker, and make sure the speaker knows the level of the audience.

* Be sure to have the students send a thank-you note.

* As a special public relations tactic, notify the system's publicity department to come for pictures.

* Consider sending the speaker's immediate supervisor a note commending the speaker for generously granting time to such a task. Thank the boss, too, for being kind enough to release the speaker for the visit, if that's the case.

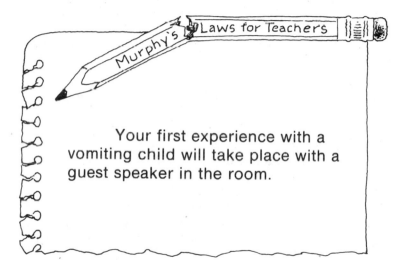

Murphy's Laws for Teachers

Your first experience with a vomiting child will take place with a guest speaker in the room.

h

health: physical and mental

* While this is probably written policy in most schools, we feel that it is important enough to point out here:

1. Do not keep medicine in class.
2. Do not administer medicine to a student or allow students to administer it to themselves.
3. Send all medicines and accompanying notes from home to the office or clinic.

* Review health cards or cumulative folders to make yourself aware of any physical or mental health problems in your classroom. Inform any person who must be in charge of your students of these problems. Alert anyone with a need to know.

* Be especially alert to problems that may be aggravated by strenuous physical activity. PE specialists need to know children's health problems before their first meeting with the students.

* Be sure that new physical or mental health problems are entered on students' health cards or in the cumulative folders.

* Any child wearing glasses or having a hearing problem may need special seating. Handle this as discreetly as possible. If you are not sure where the best location for the student is, ask the parents to check with their doctor. Tell the kids that they may move whenever they have difficulty seeing or hearing.

* Make special provisions for a child with elimination problems to be excused whenever the need arises. You should be informed of the condition in a note from a doctor or from home, not in a verbal message from the child. File any note of this kind in the student's cumulative folder for safekeeping.

* If a student's health problem is a severe one, such as epilepsy, heart trouble, or a fatal allergic reaction, familiarize yourself with emergency treatment for the condition.

* If a student has a physical condition that could require special equipment or medication, be sure that it is available to the student. For example, if a student is allergic to bee stings, make sure the clinic has a bee sting kit.

* Prepare your students for any type of health testing to be done in school. This might include scoliosis screening, vision and hearing screening, annual height and weight checks, heart scans, checks for head lice, or routine dental checkups. Being prepared helps to allay fears.

* If you detect an unpleasant odor on a student, possibly urine or stale perspiration, and you are unable to broach the subject with the student, send the student to the nurse for consultation.

* Watch for scratching or other signs of skin irritation. A rash that does not disappear and that the kid doesn't explain could be scabies. Send the kid to the nurse.

* If asked, be able to give information about the community health resources available to students and their families.

* Varicose veins is a common ailment among teachers. To avoid varicose veins:

1. Wear good support hose.
2. Purchase a hard rubber runner or a good rug with a thick mat to put in front of the chalkboard. This will cushion some of the hard wear and tear your legs are taking.
3. Wear crepe-soled shoes.

4. Whenever you sit down between or after classes, prop up your feet.

* If your school system does not require you to have a tuberculin test, get one anyway. Students are not required to have a tuberculin test for admittance to some school systems—which is all the more reason for you to be checked.

* Another common ailment is urinary tract infection, probably caused by infrequent urination. Take the time to hit the restroom and drink plenty of water.

* For related topics see **behavior problems, child abuse, safety,** and **stress.**

homework

* Keep these words in mind:

1. *Who?* If the students are adults in continuing education, don't assign gobs of work, because they may have full-time jobs.
2. *What?* Know the objective of the homework assignment and make sure the kids know it too.
3. *When?* If it's football or baseball season, try to remember what it was like when you were a kid. If it's the day before a field day, be a sport.
4. *Why?* If it serves no purpose other than to give the class something to do, skip it.
5. *How much?* If five problems will tell you as much as twenty-five, go with five.
6. *Materials needed?* Will all the necessary resources to complete the assignment be available to every student at home?

* Do not assign homework for punishment.

* Ask for feedback from your students on the amount and the nature of homework. Ask for feedback from the parents, too.

* Parents usually have questions about your homework policy. Have a specific policy concerning homework assignments and inform parents and students of this policy.

* Never accept the responsibility of writing down a kid's assignments. Don't encourage a parent to accept the responsibility of the completion of homework assignments by initialing the assignment before it returns to school, either. Make the responsibility of writing down and completing homework assignments totally the student's.

* Not all families have access to magazines at home, nor do all families subscribe to newspapers. Be prepared to make other arrangements if you make assignments concerning the use of magazines or newspapers.

honor roll

* Make the honor roll a big deal for your students who qualify. Recognize these students with:

1. personal congratulatory notes
2. names posted in the classroom, main hall, guidance office, or main office
3. an article written about them in the school paper
4. an article written about them in the classroom paper
5. a special pin to wear for the day
6. a special club or organization to recognize these students
7. an award on Awards Day at the end of the year

* Make certain that the students and their parents know the exact criteria for being included on the honor roll. Put the criteria in writing and give the list to other teachers, to parents, and to students.

* Once the standards for making the honor roll have been set, make no exceptions.

* Check periodically on these students who are capable of making the honor roll. If a particular area may keep them from making the honor roll, inform them of the area and perhaps offer suggestions for improvement.

i

ideas

* Keep 3 x 5 cards with you at all times to make notes.

* Have a get-together for sharing ideas or suggest it as a possible in-service workshop at your school. Each participant must bring one idea pertaining to a specific topic.

* Be flexible enough to correlate activities from one subject to another. If you had planned to show a film on Benjamin Franklin but the projector goes on the blitz at the start of your social studies period, check your language arts lesson for today and see if you can work in Benjamin Franklin there. Surely you could tie in old Ben with a creative writing or descriptive writing assignment. If the projector is fixed later, show the film during language arts.

* For bulletin board ideas, walk through your own school with your 3 x 5 cards in hand and sketch pictures of your colleagues' bulletin boards. These can be filed in a box or pasted in a notebook. (See **notebooks**.)

* Keep samples of kids' art work from year to year as suggestions for projects for next year.

* Ask your librarian if you may help clean out the old magazine file and take a stack of magazines for your class.

* Make a habit of browsing through coloring books. Often, a very simple picture can spark a new bulletin board idea.

* Books for kids at discount stores and supermarkets are excellent sources of ideas. Books on simple science experiments, on animals of all sorts, and on crafts and hobbies are a fine way to build up your idea file. They are tax deductible, and yours to cut up as you like.

* Make it a point to scan the professional magazines regularly for new teaching and bulletin board ideas.

* For related topics see bulletin boards, opaque projector, and resources.

in-service

* Don't hesitate to be the one in your school to suggest topics for in-service. If there is an area in which you need assistance (for instance, discipline, communication, or study skills), suggest that your school plan an in-service on the topic. You must remember, however, that if you make nifty suggestions, you'll probably be asked to head the committee.

* If you hear a good speaker, get all the information you can and try to secure the speaker for an in-service. For example, we heard a police detective speak at a university. We were so impressed by the talk on child abuse that we plan to engage the detective for an in-service at our school.

* Check with teachers at other schools to find out what they have planned for in service. Meaningless in-services are boring and a waste of valuable time, and they can contribute to teacher burnout and stress. Make them meaningful for yourself and for others.

* Do a little research to find what other systems have done in the way of in-services. Professional magazines often contain articles about timely topics for in-services.

* After each in-service program, ask for an evaluation from the faculty. Pass the good ideas on to other schools and ax the poor ones.

instruction

Lesson plans are the basis for instruction. While we have heard of people who were super teachers without plans at all, we have never seen this phenomenon firsthand and tend not to believe that such people exist.

* Your lesson plans are an important factor in your evaluation. Make sure your lesson plans are well thought out, varied, and comprehensive. Many administrators collect plan books at the end of the school year; they may also ask to see them periodically during the school year. Keep your plan book up to date.

* Make sure your plans are so well constructed that another teacher could write your substitute's plans if you were unexpectedly absent.

* Capitalize on the moment. One teacher we know pulls the shades when it snows so that the class can continue to work quietly without distraction. How sad! The drawn window shade does not keep the child in all of us from daydreaming about the snow. Instead, we open our shades wider, have the kids turn their desks to face the windows, and capitalize on the event. The students write haiku poetry about snow, draw pictures of animals whose camouflage is affected by the snow, talk about the effect of a heavy snowfall on the feeding of birds, or simply daydream with a good recording playing in the background. Other moments to capitalize on include:

> storms
> holidays
> school events (PE shows, elections, a special lunch)
> sirens (ambulances, police cars, and fire trucks)
> workers in your classroom
> workers outside the room but visible to your class
> days important to class members (birthdays, new babies, being adopted)

Make such occasions interesting to the children and easy on yourself. Go with the situation; don't fight it.

* If you aren't sure about a fact, don't teach it until you *are* sure. Learning is difficult enough; unlearning is more difficult.

* Praise work well done—verbally, nonverbally, or in writing.

* Allow students time for logical thinking. Ask thought-provoking questions.

* Guide students to develop their senses of humor, honesty, and fair play by setting an example.

* Build up every child's ego a little every day. An extremely slow learner may smile for an hour if you merely praise his or her paper heading.

* Have every child's attention before giving directions. Then use a minimum of words.

* If you lose the class's interest, change pace *orally.* This may be the time to insert a little humor or encourage student participation. Keep interest in your lessons high by often involving kids in discussions, experiments, board work, or hands-on activities.

* For related topics see **assignments, communication: oral, directions, lesson plans,** and **plan book.**

j

janitor

* Don't leave a real mess for the janitor at the end of the day. Have your students get in the habit of:

1. clearing books from the floor
2. placing chairs on top of tables
3. cleaning the floor of trash
4. closing and locking windows
5. leveling window shades
6. washing chalkboards
7. watering plants
8. setting trash cans near the door for easy emptying

* If a student can do a job easily and safely, don't make the janitor do it.

* Refer to all custodial workers respectfully by their last names—Mr. Salisbury, Ms. Hathaway.

jargon

Avoid using educational abbreviations (jargon) when speaking to parents or other persons outside of the profession. If you must use an abbreviation or special term, take the time to explain exactly what it means.

jobs

* Never do anything you can get a kid to do. They love to help. Jobs that kids love to do are:

1. cleaning chalkboards and desks
2. distributing or collecting books or papers
3. returning borrowed items to the library or other resource centers
4. filing
5. sorting
6. running messages (they like this one best)
7. acting as line or hall monitors
8. cleaning tables in the lunchroom
9. watering plants
10. feeding animals
11. securing PE equipment

    * Have a job chart and change responsibilities often—about once a week seems to satisfy the students' need to help.

    * Since some jobs are favorite jobs to have and others are considered yucky (feeding the animals is great, but cleaning the lunchroom tables is awful), make certain that everyone has a shot at each of the jobs.

    * Put the name of each student on a 3 x 5 card. Pile the cards in a deck. Every time you need to assign a classroom job, pick a card from the top of the deck. That student gets the job. This eliminates labeling jobs as either female jobs or male jobs.

At this point we are considering LD resource as opposed to LD self-contained. According to PL 94-142, these placements are within the parameters of the law. Your child's disfluency would be minimized by regular classes with the speech pathologist in addition to the special education placement. Now that this has been explained, will you please sign the IEP?

kissing and public displays of affection

Even though there is usually a strict policy concerning kissing and public displays of affection, junior- and senior-high-school students tend to ignore the policy. As much as you'd like to be lenient, you must enforce the policy. Realize that warm weather really does bring on greater frequency of hand holding, kissing, and hugging and be more alert when spring approaches.

labeling

* Early in the year, give each student a positive label. Say—and mean it—"You are the best _____ I've ever known!" This positive image will give students a basis from which to grow and may be the only positive thing they've heard in years. You may see them move from this positive statement into other areas where they may excel. Reinforce each of these new positives when you can by mentioning it to them, to their parents, and to their classmates.

* For related topics see **self-concept** and **sex equity.**

law

Laws covering schools and children mention the Latin phrase *in loco parentis,* which translates to "in the place of the parent." This means that you are the surrogate parent while a student is in your care. If an accident befalls the child while he or she is in your care and the parents decide to sue for negligence, your case may rest on whether you did what a parent would have done for the child. Keep these areas in mind:

1. *Proper instruction.* You have talked to the students about and posted rules governing behavior and the use of materials and equipment.

2. *Adequate supervision.* You have been directed never to leave your class, but if you must leave, see that they are adequately supervised by a teacher in the next room. Do not stay a minute longer than you absolutely

have to. Make sure you leave the students seated and busy and with instructions to stay seated.

3. *Safe premises.* Check each day for hazards in the classroom and on the playground. Avoid premises that are potentially dangerous—playing areas near highways, for example.

* Accidents do happen. Be able to prove that you took the proper precautions to prevent the accident.

* If a ball goes off the school grounds, *you* get it, or send another adult for it. Do not send a kid for it. If a child is injured, a court of law may not think that you were acting in a prudent manner if you sent the child off the school grounds to retrieve a ball.

* Never dismiss a student to run a noneducational errand. If you send a student down the hall to your best friend's room with a newsy note and the kid falls and chips a tooth, the essence of the note will probably be revealed to determine the urgency of the child having to deliver it. That might be difficult to justify.

* Check into securing a teacher liability policy as an addendum to your homeowners policy. This policy provides a great deal of security for less than ten dollars per year. Most liability insurance policies will pay legal fees to represent you if you are taken to court in a school-related matter. Most teacher liability policies will not cover you if you physically abuse a child. A *tort* in law means a "wrong." It is not a chocolate pastry in layers. Your teacher liability policy may be referred to as "tort insurance."

lesson plans

* Well-developed plans are the basis of good teaching. Good plans can help you to achieve good classroom management, discipline, good instruction and an easier life.

* Lesson plans are guides; they are not written in blood. Be flexible. If a situation arises that could be a

magnificent learning experience but you have not included it in your lesson plans for the day, our advice is to chance it. Later, if you are asked why you are not following your plans, your enthusiasm and logical reason will certainly be sufficient. Make up the lesson you lost in the very near future.

    * At the beginning of the year, key what the abbreviations or Roman numerals in your plans stand for. We have found using "I" for our objectives, "II" for the procedure to be followed, and "III" for evaluation to be an effective shortcut in writing lesson plans. A sample plan follows:

Spelling 9:30–9:50

  I Vowel /e/
 II Teacher's edition, p. 73
     Introduce new words orally with discussion
     Answer questions orally, p. 74
     Assign p. 75 #1–8 Homework
III Teacher observation

    * Keep detailed lesson plans. They are a definite record of what you taught and when you taught it. You may need proof someday.

    * Have lesson plans ready to go and on your desk before you leave in the afternoon. Try to stay a week ahead in your plans.

    * For related topics see **assignments, objectives, plan book,** and **substitutes.**

lining up

    Lining up in an orderly manner and walking to your destination quietly ensures that the class will be orderly for you or whoever is to take charge.

    * Set the procedure for having students line up and walk to a destination the very first day of school. Plan stops along the way so kids don't get away from you.

✱ For some reason, being first in line is a biggie with kids. Use it to your advantage. Let the best of whatever line up first as a reward.

✱ Lining up is something we can all master. Help students feel better by verbally rewarding them when they do it well.

✱ The first few steps under **behavior problems** (see **behavior problems**) all apply to lining up as well. Your class and you are being observed and evaluated every day in lines going here and there in school. Be in shape early in the year.

listening

✱ Make sure your speaking speed does not exceed the children's listening speed. If you see bewildered faces or receive bored yawns, you may be going too fast. Slow down.

✱ Brainstorm with older children to arrive at your own list of good listening techniques. Make a poster of the techniques they listed—stated positively, of course. This makes them more aware of listening and more responsible to the task.

✱ Be a good listener yourself. Don't fake it—the kid will sense it.

✱ Establish a listening purpose before your lectures, films, tapes, or guest speakers. A number of questions could be written on the chalkboard prior to the activity. Students then listen to find the answers to each question. For example, prior to a film for language arts, the following questions could be used:

1. *Who* is the hero/heroine?
2. *What* was the major problem?
3. *Where* did the story take place?
4. *When* did the story take place?
5. *How* was the problem solved?
6. *Who* solved the problem?

✱ When you are listening, try to pick up the person's nonverbal message also.

* Have absolute quiet and attention (not always the same thing) before taking roll, giving directions, giving assignments, or making announcements.

* For related topics see **communication: oral** and **directions**.

living things

* Use extreme caution before introducing a living thing other than a nice philodendron to your class. Kids poke, animals bite or escape in the school building, and you're responsible. Consider another viewpoint: Is it fair to subject the animal to this life?

* Animal bites should be treated immediately. Send the bitten kid to the nurse or office, notify the kid's parents, and inform Animal Control if necessary.

lost and found

* Label all items that are yours and encourage students to do the same.

* *Every* Friday, have the kids take home their coats, sweaters, mittens, boots, lunch boxes, and book bags. This will save you from having a well-stocked lost and found in June. Better still, you will never be faced with the odor of three-day old egg salad at eight-thirty Monday morning.

So you're planning on taking it all home in one trip?!

m

make-up work

* Inform students how make-up work is to be handled in the first week of school.
* Encourage students to take down phone numbers of other students who will inform them of homework assignments and school news on the days when they are absent.
* If possible, encourage students to find someone in the class who lives near them and would be willing to bring home any materials they need when they are absent.
* Keep a make-up work folder to fill with assignments for absentees. Include dittos, handouts, and messages.
* Have a kid with decent handwriting copy all the assignments into a notebook, which is dated day by day. When kids are absent, make it their responsibility to go to the notebook, copy assignments, and complete the work assigned.

maps

* Turn a wall map to the wall for a perfect movie screen.
* To make an identification test out of a map quickly, tape a piece of clear plastic over the map and write numbers on it.
* Preserve paper maps from magazines by laminating them or covering them with clear contact paper.

✻ Use a laminated map and play "Where in the World Are You?" with older kids by giving them the longitudinal and latitudinal points and having them find the place. Then do the reverse—give them a place name and ask for the longitudinal and latitudinal points.

✻ To use the maps in a textbook more effectively, supply the class with sheets of clear plastic. Placing these over the maps in their textbooks, students can make special marks as visual aids for themselves. These sheets can be reused many times if students write on them with grease pencils or crayons. They can be wiped clean with a wet paper towel.

mental health

(See health: physical and mental)

money and valuables

✻ The price of this book is deductible. So are other materials you buy to use at school. Save all receipts.

✻ Courses you take for credit for certification are tax deductible.

✻ Keep your charge cards in a separate container and not in your wallet. A person rummaging

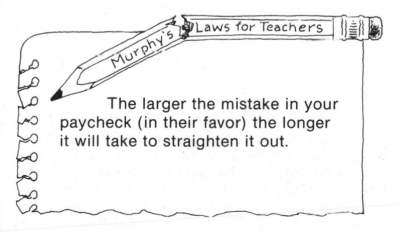

Murphy's Laws for Teachers

The larger the mistake in your paycheck (in their favor) the longer it will take to straighten it out.

through your purse is probably looking for money and will grab your wallet. If you don't carry great gobs of money in your wallet and your charge cards aren't in there, you'll not have lost much more than a few dollars and the cost of a wallet. It's a real pain, however, to lose charge cards.

* If you have a file cabinet or desk drawer that locks, use it for your valuables. It is still good to form the habit of taking your wallet or purse with you wherever you go.

* Don't bring to school anything you really would hate to lose.

* Advise the children also to keep their treasured items at home. While Grandma's 200-year-old Indian vase is a great item for show and tell (alias "bring and brag") it cannot possibly be replaced if you or a student smash it.

* Don't hold students' money, watches, jewelry, or purses, because you are responsible for their loss or breakage.

* When collecting money from students, be accurate, give receipts, and turn in the money to the office as soon as possible.

* Encourage kids not to leave money in class. In fact, encourage them not to bring large amounts of cash to school for any reason.

* Suggest that students pay by check whenever possible. In any event, collect money the first thing in the day, before a check or cash is lost.

* If a youngster in the early grades comes to school with an unusually large amount of money, check it out. A phone call to the home is probably in order.

motivation

Understand at the outset of your teaching career that you cannot make someone else learn. You can set up optimum conditions for students to learn, but it is still their choice to learn or not to learn.

* Spark an interest for the topic you are about to teach. If the student sees absolutely no need to learn what you are teaching, the student's learning process is closed down. However, if you can somehow make students see how learning about a subject can benefit them throughout their lives—and make them believe it and remember it—you've got them half taught. When there is a need to know, learning (and teaching) is a cinch.

* Be enthusiastic. It's contagious.

music

* Be aware that music is social history. "Over There" is a product of World War I, "Brother, Can You Spare a Dime?" is from the Depression era, and "Nine to Five" is about a 1980s issue—harassment on the job. Incorporate music in your lesson plans as a change of pace. There are excellent recordings produced to correlate with social studies and language arts lessons throughout the grades.

* Choose a popular record (one you have listened to beforehand) to play for your class. Then ask questions for listening skills. What do the lyrics mean? How does the music create a feeling in the listener?

* Have a radio in your classroom and find a station that plays programmed music—the kind you hear in supermarkets and doctors' offices—or collect tapes or records of easy-listening music. Then, while your class is working on a quiet project, treat them to five or ten minutes of music. This works nicely the day before vacation.

* Capitalize on all the children who take music lessons on any instrument and let them play for you and the class. This is a terrific ego booster for the kid and a good motivator for the other children.

* Conduct exercises accompanied by a rousing record for indoor physical education on a rainy day. This definitely provides a change of pace.

—n—

new kids

* Make up several folders for the new kids you may receive during the year. In the folder, include a map of the school with the important places marked, a list of the teachers the student must know, a schedule of classes, rules of the classroom, library information, supplies needed, extracurricular activities, homework policy, absentee policy, school calendar, supply store information, bus information, lunchroom policy, and withdrawal procedure (just in case).

* Assign the new kid a buddy for the first few days so that the buddy can introduce the new kid around. Try to choose a buddy who rides the new kid's bus.

* Ask an aide to help the new student for the first few days until the student has adjusted.

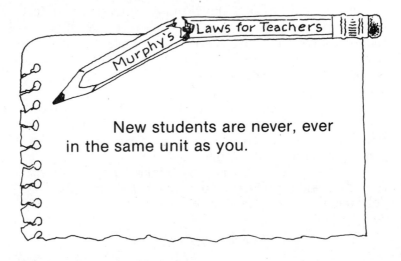

Murphy's Laws for Teachers

New students are never, ever in the same unit as you.

newspapers

* For your sake and for the kids' sake, if there is something your students have done well, *tell them!* Also tell it to the building administrators, to the school through the school newspaper, to the system through the newsletter, to the community through the monthly bulletin, or to the world through the press.

* Encourage production of a regular newspaper as part of your language program or as an extracurricular activity in upper grades. Have kids take the paper home to share with their families.

* When kids or their relatives make the news, make a big deal out of it. (Good news only, please!)

* Encourage students of all ages to use the newspaper and to bring in articles of interest for discussion. You can use the newspaper to teach math, social studies, current affairs, language, and spelling and as a resource for projects.

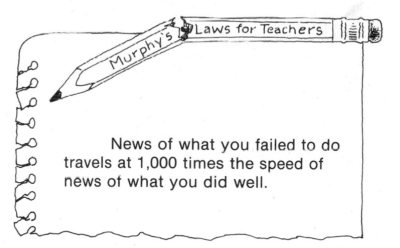

Murphy's Laws for Teachers

News of what you failed to do travels at 1,000 times the speed of news of what you did well.

notebooks

* Set standards for keeping notebooks the very first week and remind the students of them throughout the year. Some examples of standards are:

1. Each entry must be legibly written.
2. Pages may not be torn out or skipped.
3. Write notes for only one subject in each notebook.
4. Have items in the proper order.
5. Write on both sides of the page.

　　　* Use notebooks for different subjects. Having a different colored notebook for each subject and keeping orderly notes teaches kids organization and responsibility for one's belongings.
　　　* Instruct kids to include the following in their notebooks:

　　　class notes
　　　notes from outside readings
　　　homework assignments
　　　class assignments
　　　graded tests (pasted in)
　　　dittos (pasted in)
　　　newspaper or magazine articles
　　　drawings

　　　* The notebook is a great way to find out about the quality of the kid's work and can be a great conference item. Collect and examine notebooks periodically.
　　　* For a quick check of who has what in their notebooks, simply make up quiz questions from notes your kids *should* have in their notebooks. Make it an "open notebook" quiz.
　　　* Keep a notebook for faculty meetings. Write in it the stuff that pertains to you or your kids.

O

objectives

* Write objectives in behavioral terms, but be brief. For example, write "Identify the /m/ sound." Every teacher's manual we have reviewed lately includes objectives for the lessons. All you need to do is copy these objectives into your lesson plan book in a shortened form.

* Purchase a yellow marker and underline the objectives for your lessons in your teacher's manual.

* Make your students familiar with the word *objective*. State your objectives before each lesson; just before dismissal, review what you taught during the day. Use the word *objectives* as you do this.

* On dittos, write the objective right at the top. If you are using a prepared ditto, look at the bottom for the objective written on it. If the objective is not written, ask the students to determine what the objective of the ditto is and to write it on their answer sheet.

* Point out the objectives as you review papers with parents at conference time. Objectives can help you make parents aware of their children's strengths and weaknesses.

* For related topics see **goals** and **lesson plans**.

opaque projector

* Make the opaque projector your friend! Use it to create bulletin boards. For example, a small, outlined coloring book picture blown up to 2 feet by 3 feet makes an instant bulletin board figure.

* Kids from about grade 3 and up can use the opaque projector to copy a picture. Then they can color it, cover it in clear contact paper, and cut it out.

* Use tag board if you're copying using an opaque projector. It's thinner, cheaper and easier to work with than poster board.

* If the picture you want to enlarge is very tiny, blow it up once and copy it. Then blow up the copy to the size you want.

* *Caution:* Don't place slick paper magazines and encyclopedia pages under an opaque projector. They'll burn.

open house

Your school's open house is your chance to give parents the impression of you that you want them to have. Often, messages go home via the students that paint a very distorted picture of classroom life.

* Encourage parents to attend open house in these ways:

1. Plan the date well: Avoid nights on which big ball games or functions at other area schools are scheduled. Also avoid nights that are close to holidays.
2. Have students write invitations.
3. Publish the date in the newspaper, in the school's monthly bulletin, or in the community newsletter.
4. Announce it on the PA system.
5. Have the dates printed in the student handbook.
6. Provide baby-sitting services.
7. Ask PTA members to make phone calls to remind parents of the date.

* Make your room welcome to visiting parents in these ways:

1. Make the room clean, orderly, and interesting.
2. Create attractive and purposeful bulletin boards.
3. Display students' work.
4. Display materials and equipment.

* Consider having all the specialists and clubs in school set up displays in central locations so parents can visit them.

* Use the open house to tell parents you want to work with them. Set the cooperative mood that will allow the best efforts from their children. Stand at the door and greet parents in a friendly way. Be prepared with what you want to say. Display a positive attitude toward the new year. Invite suggestions.

* Since you obviously cannot have a conference with every parent who attends the open house, have a conference sheet on your desk and ask interested parents to sign up for conferences at a convenient time.

* If you notice you have hangers-on who are waiting around for everyone else to leave so they can have a conference, tell them that it is unfair to them and to their children for you to comment without being prepared for a conference. Assure them that you do want to see them, but at a more convenient time. Be firm. Arrange a later conference or explain how conferences are set up in your school.

p

pacing

Pacing requires preparation and organization on your part. Once preparation is done, stress is minimized. You know how much material needs to be covered, how much time you have to cover the material, where your materials are, and when they are to be used.

✱ Check your teacher's manuals thoroughly—many of them include suggestions as to how long it should take you to cover text material. If a teacher's manual does not recommend a time scheme, divide the number of text pages by the number of teaching days to determine how much should be covered each day. Of course, given the fact that you are expected to individualize instruction, you must make allowances for

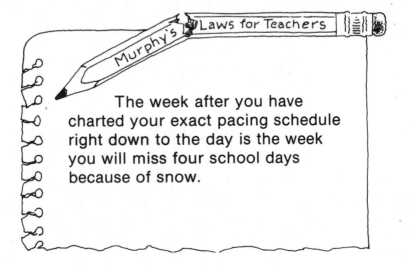

Murphy's Laws for Teachers

The week after you have charted your exact pacing schedule right down to the day is the week you will miss four school days because of snow.

the slower students in terms of the quantity or quality of work required as well as for the more gifted students for whom you must plan enrichment or challenge work.

* Pacing also involves three strategies:

1. Plan lessons so that you end one well before another begins. A smooth transition from one subject to another aids in classroom control.

2. Leave enough time to clean up art activities. It may take as long as fifteen minutes.

3. Combine directions to move swiftly from one activity to another. We had math, then lunch, and then social studies scheduled one year, so just before lunch, we directed the students to put their math materials away and to get their lunch boxes and social studies materials ready. After the third week of school, when math was over, the students automatically followed this procedure.

* Don't have projects all due on the day before report cards go home, since you have to grade the projects before you can average grades. Likewise, test different subjects or classes on different days in order to spread your work out.

* For related topics see **audio-visual aids, daily reminder file, stress,** and **time management.**

paper flow

Work out a complete system for paper flow in your room. Organize and implement it right at the start of the year.

Collecting Papers

* Secure and label an IN basket (a large shirt box works nicely) for each subject or class period you teach. Students will know exactly where to put papers unless you direct them otherwise.

* Assign a specific student to collect and alphabetize papers before you receive them. Alphabetically ordered papers make for easy recording of grades and easy finding of a specific student's paper.

* Consider assigning students' numbers in alphabetical order. (Most grade book lines are numbered, and you want the kid on that line to have that number, obviously.) When students head their papers, have them include the numbers next to their names, preferably in the upper right-hand corner, so the papers can be ordered numerically. Easy?

Distribution of Papers

* For best control, designate a paper person and let the job of paper distribution be that kid's alone. Fewer kids up and moving about means less confusion.

* The best person to give out graded papers is *you*. Be aware of children's feelings when handing back their papers.

Recording Papers

* Alphabetize papers or numerically order them to make recording grades easier, faster, and more accurate. More accurate, you say? Yeah, because hippity-hopping from A to M to D to X is hard on the eyeballs. Moving your eyes down a continuous line helps you to get the grade in the right box.

* Slide a ruler down a grade book page as you fill in grades; this will improve accuracy.

Storing Papers

* Visit the local ice cream store and ask the owner for about thirty of those enormous cylindrical ice cream containers. These can be painted, decorated, and labeled to serve as mailboxes for easy distribution of papers. The cartons can be stapled together in a pyramidal shape to save space.

paper headings

* Establish a set way that you want every paper headed. Demand that every paper have this heading, and have students correct papers that have improper headings. Suggest that your method (or some other satisfactory method) be the schoolwide standard. This

will make it easier for the students as they move up through the grades, as there will be some continuity.

* The heading should include the student's name (first and last), number (see **paper flow**), date, subject, text, and page or type of work. You might also want them to include the objective of the assignment (see **objectives**).

* Make an enormous bulletin board showing how papers coming to you are to be headed. Such a board is perfect for the first of the year and easy to construct. And it saves on the vocal cords!

parties

* Let the students assume as much responsibility for the planning, preparing, serving, and cleaning up after a party as they are able to handle.

* Insist that students follow this rule: If they have drinks on their desks, they are not allowed to leave their desks. Once things to eat and drink have been cleared away, then students can move about.

* We received this neat party idea from an inventive colleague. Have a sundae bar! Let the students brainstorm and think of all the things they could put on ice cream: bananas, cherries, sauces, chocolate, nuts, marshmallows, whipped cream. Have the planning committee bring in as many items as they like. They should provide paper bowls, plastic spoons, and napkins. On party day, order ice cream cups from the cafeteria, dump the contents into the paper bowls, and let the students select whatever they want to make their own sundaes. Clean up with a huge, plastic trash bag.

* Modify the above idea to a salad bar or a sandwich bar, with students bringing in different appropriate ingredients. How about a health food bar? A cheese bar? A fruit bar? A foreign food bar?

physical education

* Know all the health limitations of students in your class and inform those persons who need to know

about these limitations (PE specialist, aide, art teacher, librarian).

✳ PE is the accident time of the day. Instruct the class ahead of time exactly what you want them to do in case you must escort a class member to the clinic or office.

✳ Encourage your students to dress appropriately for the activities you have planned for them. Good sturdy running shoes are a must for PE.

✳ Prior to using any gym or game equipment, instruct your class in the correct use of equipment.

✳ Have an alternate plan for PE in case the weather changes. Students who are lined up to go outside but find out that it's raining are in no mood to stand quietly waiting for you to rummage around in idea books to come up with something to do. Don't forget to leave contingency plans for the substitute.

✳ Participate in PE. Exercise, run, and play the games with your students. The kids think it's neat, and it's good for your physical and mental health. Besides, physical activity helps to eliminate stress. Keep comfortable shoes at school for such activities.

✳ For a related topic see safety.

physical health

(See health: physical and mental.)

placement in special programs

✳ Do not suggest to parents that their children need special programs. That decision is up to the specialists after testing. Parents get upset (and rightly so) when one person tells them one thing, and then, after testing is completed, they are told another.

✳ Be as thorough as you can when filling out forms for a child's placement in a special program. Try to present a clear and true picture of that child. Keep in mind that the student's admittance to a special program is to help the student, which is your essential job.

   * In filling out the forms for special placement, describe actual behavior. It is not necessary to interpret the child's behavior or to otherwise assert your opinion.

   * Be especially careful to avoid educational jargon when talking to parents about special programs. (See jargon.)

plan book

   * Go through your plan book and, using the systemwide calendar, mark out all the holidays. Using your school calendar, mark due dates for progress reports, report cards, PTA meetings, in-service program days, conference days, records days, and the first and last days of school.

   * As you receive monthly or weekly calendars, mark in your plan book items that pertain to you specifically. Then post the calendar to save questions. Any changes in your time schedule will change the time you have to teach, and your lessons need to be changed accordingly. Note also absences of resource people and remember to tell the students who may be affected. (For example, "Nancy, No SCA meeting today." We find that writing down these personal messages helps us and the students to remember.

   * Use your plan book as a guide; feel free to be flexible. We used to hear a lot about the "teachable moment"—that golden minute that wasn't written in your plans but was the very instant you had sparked your students to really learn something. Go with it, but note in your plans what you did teach and plan to catch up on what you missed the next day.

   * Make dittos of a set of empty facing pages in your plan book. Fill in on the dittos the things that are fixed for each day or each week: PE, lunch, homeroom, bathroom breaks, art, music, planning periods, study halls, duty assignments. Run off copies and paste them over the original pages in your plan book. This saves

hours of needless repetition. You'll end up doing all your lesson planning at school because your pasted-in plan book now weighs a ton!

    * Color-code special events in your plan book: specialists in purple, films in green, planning times in red.

    * Note any special things you have to do for that day—conferences, items due, appointments—near the place where you start your day.

	VARIED 9:00 - 9:50	SOCIAL STUDIES 9:50 - 10:30	MATH 10:30 - 11:25	P.E.	SCIENCE HEALTH 12:00-12:30	L	SPELLING LANGUAGE 1:15 - 2:00	READING 2:00 - 2:50	
MONDAY	MUSIC MR. POHLE 9:00 - 9:45	I II — III	I II ① — III I II ② — III	AREA 2 ME 11:25 -12:00	I II — III	ENTER SIDE 1	I II — III I II — III	I II ① — III I II ② — III	**MONDAY**
TUESDAY	ART MS. PARKER 9:00- 9:45	I II — III	I II ① — III I II ② — III	AREA 1 ME 11:25 - 12:00	I II — III	ENTER SIDE 1	I II — III I II — III	I II ① — III I II ② — III	**TUESDAY**
WEDNESDAY	LIBRARY AVAILABLE 9:00 -9:30 HAND- WRITING	I II — III	I II ① — III I II ② — III	AREA 2 MRS. MATIKA	I II — III	AREA 2	I II — III I II — III	I II ① — III I II ② — III	**WEDNESDAY**
THURSDAY	SCIENCE I II — III	I II — III	I II ① — III I II ② — III	SPECIALIST	I II — III	12:30 - 1:00	I II — III I II — III	I II ① — III I II ② — III	**THURSDAY**
FRIDAY	SCIENCE I II — III	I II — III	I II ① — III I II ② — III	AREA 3 MR. McCART	I II — III	LUNCH	I II — III I II — III	I II ① — III I II ② — III	**FRIDAY**

Sample Dittos of Lesson Plan Book Pages

* Make your plan book a readable record of what you have taught. If you are ever questioned about what you taught on a specific day, your plan book should be an indication. Some school systems use a teacher's plan book as part of the evaluation process.

* For related topics see **assignments, audio-visual aids, instruction, lesson plans, objectives,** and **pacing.**

policies

* Read them and know them—or know where to find them—because ignorance is no excuse. In education, if you're thinking of doing it, there's a policy about it somewhere. There are federal policy, state policy, school system policy, and individual school policy, and there are handbooks or policy books to cover them all. Locate these policy books early in the year.

* Situations are easier to handle if there are written and published guidelines. If you feel your school's policy is lacking, don't hesitate to initiate additions to it. Likewise, if you feel a policy is antiquated, don't hesitate to request its change or removal.

* Familiarize yourself with the following school policies:

1. Who has the right to view student records?
2. Who has final say on communications emanating from the school?
3. May students be searched and, if so, by whom?
4. To whom can students be released from school?
5. What are the rights of noncustodial parents in regard to school matters?

professional library books

* Ask for books as gifts, check flea markets and yard sales for them, ask for library discards, or choose free books from your students' book club.

* If you are taking courses, check the professional library in your school for the textbook you need. Many teachers donate used college textbooks to their own schools, and you could borrow them for the duration of your class, saving the price of purchase. With any luck, you'll find important points already underlined and super notes in the margins.

projects

* Make sure a project is a fun way to learn. Students don't learn much if they cry every time they have to work on a project because it frustrates them.

* Know the socio-economic level of the student's family. If the project you are planning will place a hardship on the family, don't assign it to be done at home. Scour up materials and have the project completed at school.

* Consider the time of year if you assign a home-funded project. Don't assign it in September, when every tyke needs new shoes and school supplies, or in December or January, when holiday bills are sapping family wallets.

* Schedule some projects to be completed before open house so you'll have a nice display.

* Give oral, written, and illustrated guidelines whenever possible.

* Do as much of a project at school as there is time for. You want an estimate of what the children can do, not what their parents can do.

pta

* Make an effort to meet as many parents through PTA meetings as possible. This is a great way to establish a favorable rapport. Early in the year, you probably have not had difficulty with any student; therefore, your meeting with a student's parents need not broach problems. Later, if problems do occur, you

will have a favorable rapport established and will have a friendly basis for a conference.

    ✱ Education is largely a public relations business. Take part eagerly, because the more people who know you and see you in a positive light, the more people will spread the word about you and the fine things you are doing. Life becomes unbelievably easy from then on.

publicity

    ✱ Seek it! If you and your class have done something of interest, tell all! Don't be modest. Consider telling:

> administrators
> fellow teachers
> other classes
> the school paper
> the PTA newsletter
> the community newsletter
> local newspapers
> local radio stations
> local television talk shows (and national, if you dare!)
> the school system newsletter
> a trade magazine or a journal in an article written by
>   you
> your professional growth sheet

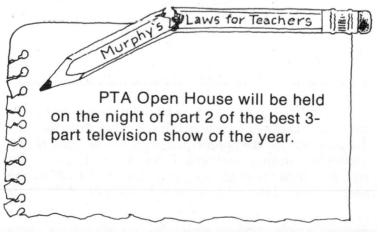

Murphy's Laws for Teachers

PTA Open House will be held on the night of part 2 of the best 3-part television show of the year.

public relations

The better the public feels about education, the more money they are willing to spend; the more money the public is willing to spend on education, the more money you will have to educate their children.

✱ Consider sending a monthly bulletin to the parents of your students explaining the objectives of the lessons you plan to teach in the coming months. Somehow, people feel less threatened when they know more about a subject. In this bulletin, you can be more specific about the things you teach. The specific objectives of the lesson are found in most teacher's manuals and how you plan to achieve those objectives is where you can be creative.

For example:

Dear Parents:

During the first month of school, the students will be learning about place value in math. We will be reading numbers up to the billions. It would be helpful if you let your child read numbers aloud to you. Have your child identify the places that numerals in a large number occupy.

Example: 456,<u>8</u>09,123   The 8 is in the <u>hundred thousands</u> place.

✱ Tell your students the names of the janitors, cafeteria workers, crossing guards, and aides so that these people may be referred to by name. Respectfully use their last names: Mr. Farrelly, Ms. Owens.

✱ Telephone parents to tell them that their child is doing quite well, or send a detailed note telling how a child excelled.

✱ Consider making an introductory phone call before the first day of school. You can set the tone for the year and assure parents that you will be available for answering questions anytime. If you do not have the time to call all the students' parents, consider calling the parents of students who are new to the school.

* If a student is sick for a few days, ask the class to send get-well notes, and send one yourself. Your thoughtfulness will help the kid want to get better.

* Talk about birthdays, new houses, moving, and new babies in the family in a positive way with students. Should parents hear of the discussions, they will appreciate your attitude.

* Summarize the day's accomplishments for the class during the five minutes before dismissal. This is a hedge against the "What did you do at school today? Aw, nothing" conversations that often take place when the students reach home.

puzzles and games

There are dozens of sources of games for kids to play at every grade level. These tips are about acquiring and caring for games and puzzles in your classroom.

* Set firm standards for using games and putting them away. Enforce these standards rigidly. Tell the students that you will not be responsible for picking up after any game or puzzle session and that if you find a piece of a game or puzzle left on the floor, the game or puzzle will be removed from the game shelf. This works. Individual abusers, if you can nab them, can be prohibited from a free game time.

* Ask your students for old games from home. This should be on a contribution basis, not on a loan basis, because you don't want to be responsible for a damaged game. Be sure the students (and their parents) understand this when they bring in the games.

* Check flea markets and yard sales for games in good condition.

* Ask friends, family members, neighbors, and retiring teachers for games they might be discarding.

* If money is available for your classroom, buy a game that all can enjoy.

* At gift-giving time, conduct a vote in your classroom to see if, instead of buying small gifts for classmates, the students would like to donate the money to buy a game or two that they might all enjoy.

* Some stores will give you a discount when you purchase games for use in the classroom.

* For color-coded puzzles, place all the pieces with the plain side up. Spray them lightly with brightly colored spray paint. Leave the pieces to dry thoroughly. Use different colors for different puzzles. When you later find stray puzzle pieces on the floor, you will know which puzzles they belong to.

* Save containers with plastic tops (frosting, butter, tea, coffee, and shortening all come in reusable containers) for storing pieces of games.

q

qualifying statements

When speaking to parents, avoid blanket statements such as, "Skip talks in school." Be specific and qualify the statement:

1. How often does he talk? Thirty times a day?
2. When does he talk—in reading, math, or science, or in lunchroom, library, or art?
3. Who, besides Skip, is affected by his talking? All?
4. Why does he talk? Boredom? Nervousness? Need for attention?

questionnaires

* Use questionnaires to gather information from students about their:

interests
conceptions of their abilities
hobbies
favorite subjects
values
likes and dislikes
vacations
career goals

* Consider using questionnaires to gather information from parents about:

1. homework policy
2. projects
3. use of free time in school

4. willingness to chaperone
5. willingness to speak on a subject in which they have expertise
6. willingness to volunteer to help with the class

quizzes
(See tests and quizzes.)

quoted . . . but misquoted
Be aware that you may be misquoted by your students to their parents. Mention this to the parents at open house and ask them to check with you if the students repeat something that really sounds weird. It's usually not so much a case of the child intentionally lying as it is of mishearing, although facts are often lost in translation.

— r —

report cards

    * Keep in mind that the report card is an evaluation of a long period of work. It is not the place to tell what David did today, and it is not the place to inform the parent for the first time that a child is misbehaving or not completing work.

    * Don't make out Brian's or Mary Alice's report cards when you are upset with them. Wait until you can be more objective. Then, when you write a comment on their report cards, start and end with a positive statement.

    * Be accurate. Take the time to check and double-check grades and comments. You are accountable numerically for every letter grade you assign.

    * Be ready to change a grade happily and with an apology if you make a mistake.

    * When you pass out report cards, encourage questions. Better to catch your mistakes now than to meet with anxious parents later.

    * If a child questions a grade, show the child the grade book. Children tend to forget the 6 Ds they earned prior to the last A. Gladly show the students their grades and let them average them for themselves. If you have mistakenly put a D where an A should be, you have already caused the child needless worry. This procedure also places the responsibility of accepting, rejecting, or questioning an evaluation on the shoulders of the student.

What positive comment can I possibly make about a paper that's a total mess and doesn't contain a single correct answer?

Diane, how nice that you completed your assignment!

* At open house, state that you appreciate any calls or notes about grades or report cards and that you will be happy to talk with any parent about any grade. Better the parent talks to you first.

* Wherever possible, on test papers and on report cards, write at least one positive comment, no matter how hard you must search.

* For a related topic see grades.

resources

* Hang around the teachers' lounge at lunch time. Listen and ask for good tips.

* When planning lessons, check the library first for books, magazines, kits, posters, filmstrips, records, and tapes to enhance your lessons.

* Expand your lessons by consulting with the art teacher, the music teacher, and the PE teacher to see if there can be some correlation between what you are teaching and activities they have planned.

* Consider finding community resources. What does your community specialize in? Our community is a predominantly military community. We have taken field trips to ships and naval installations, military bands have performed at our schools, and we've had scuba divers as speakers in our classes.

* Many persons who have no children at the school are good resources. Check newspapers for interesting persons you might invite to class for a brief lecture or demonstration.

* Parents can serve as resources in areas in which they have expertise. Include a question such as this in the information sheet that goes home at the start of the year:

Is there an area in which you'd like to share information or volunteer your time?

☐ a craft or skill _____
☐ your occupation _____
☐ foreign travel _____
☐ chaperoning _____
☐ refreshments _____
☐ typing dittos _____

* For related topics see files and ideas.

responsibilities

We give students responsibilities so that they can learn to be responsible. More responsible students exhibit more self-control. Give students as much responsibility as they can handle. Encourage parents to do the same at home.

* When students try to shift responsibility to others, guide them to accept it as their own. For example, a student who says "My parents forgot to sign my paper" should be encouraged to reword the sentence to "I forgot to get my paper signed."

* Work together with parents to teach responsibility to students. The week a kindergartener feeds the class's goldfish can be the week the child feeds the family's dog. The 4th-grader who has lunchroom duty can also assume kitchen duty at home. The home economics student can be responsible for planning family meals for a week.

✳ From the children's first school days, give them opportunities to be responsible. A kindergartener can be responsible for keeping track of personal belongings and snack money, returning signed papers, cleaning the classroom, feeding classroom pets, watering plants, or delivering messages around the school.

✳ As children grow, add to their list of responsibilities. Fourth-graders can set up and run most audio-visual equipment. They can construct bulletin boards, alphabetize papers, head committees, and organize class parties. Junior- and senior-high-school students can hold club offices, serve on school committees, participate in interscholastic competition, and select their own courses.

✳ Whatever you expect your class to be, you must be: on time, organized, prepared, cheerful, polite to all. Set a good, responsible example.

S

safety

The safety of every student is the number-one priority of every school. Make it your number-one priority, too. Keep safety standards in the minds of your students.

* Make sure the rules for the use of equipment are posted in full view, and go over them with students as necessary. Have a reminder about equipment safety written in your plans. Someday you may be called on to prove that you taught the proper use of equipment your students use.

* Plan ahead. Think what the most awful calamity is that could befall a student while performing what you have planned. If the risk is too great, skip the lesson. Weigh the worth of the lesson against the safety of the student.

* Stress proper behavior on the stairs. Caution students about slippery-soled shoes and remind them of precautions they should take on stairs.

* PE is accident time! Be there with your eyes open for a possible mishap.

* Use extra caution with bladed instruments and machines. Enforce the use of all required safety devices: gloves, goggles, safety aprons.

* If students say they are sick, let the nurse be the judge. You could easily misjudge a serious health problem. Of course, if a student wishes to make frequent visits to the clinic, that may be another problem. Look into it.

* For related topics see emergencies, field trips, health: physical and mental, and physical education.

schedules

    ✱ Post your schedule in some way every day. We use a bulletin board to post all the fixed items in our schedule, such as lunch, PE, art, music, and library time. Then we write our daily schedule on the chalkboard every day. This tends to keep children from asking you a zillion times a day, "What's next?"

    ✱ If you have a hard time remembering your schedule, keep a copy in your plan book, another in your grade book, and one taped to the top of your desk. Cover the taped copy with a sheet of clear plastic.

    ✱ To add spice to schedule-writing on the board, invest in a box of colored chalk. Write schedules on the board in different colors for different days, or write the special things you plan in different colors. Colors liven up the board.

    ✱ Include in your schedule specific times for certain things that are routinely done. The following is a sample schedule that we write on the board:

    8:50 Homeroom, buy lunch tickets, lunch count,
             silent minute, library books
    9:00 Art with specialist
    9:45 Social studies
  10:30 Math
  11:25 PE with me
  12:00 Science
  12:30 Lunch
   1:00 Story
   1:15 Language arts
   2:50 Ready for dismissal

school property

    ✱ Put your name on your stuff so it doesn't get mixed up with school property.

    ✱ Encourage students to cover their books early in the year. Check periodically to see that they are covered.

* Bookmarks are an excellent project for early in the year. Show the children how to cover a bookmark with clear contact paper and have them make one for each book they use daily. Using bookmarks discourages kids from laying open books face down, damaging the bindings. It also discourages them from using pencils or popsicle sticks and from folding corners, which damages pages.

* Whenever possible, make students sign for the materials they borrow or items they wish to take home for short periods. Have them sign an IOU for money they borrow from you. We have found that when kids sign for something, they take better care of it.

* Maintain a clean, orderly classroom. Not only does it make for good public relations when visitors or school officials drop by, it instills in students a respect for school property, for which we all pay.

seating charts

* Make a movable seating chart. On a standard 8½-by-11-inch sheet of paper, sketch your classroom desk arrangement. Make slots with a razor and insert slips of paper, each displaying the name of a student, in the appropriate desk slots. For sturdiness, paper clip the chart to a piece of cardboard. We found that students work better if they are moved frequently, but making a new seating chart is a pain. Keep your movable chart up to date and store it in a folder marked "Seating Charts" in your substitute teacher folder.

* Another kind of seating chart is an erasable one. On a plain sheet of paper, sketch your classroom desk arrangement. Cover the sheet with a clear plastic overlay and use a grease pencil to label the kids' names on the desks. When you feel a change is necessary, wipe the name from one desk and write it on another. Make two or three charts with different seating arrangements. Try rows, circles, and groups for variety.

self-concept

Children who feel good about themselves feel free to try new things and to express new ideas. Work at creating situations in which students can feel good about themselves.

* Put up a map of the United States or a map of the world and have the children place their names on the map to show where they were born.

* Have kids make self-portraits to let down some self-consciousness barriers. You should make one, too. Everyone seems to get a good hoot out of this activity.

* Encourage the school librarian to buy some of the numerous books available on building self-concept. Consider one self-concept–building activity for your students daily. Do this for them and for yourself.

* Maintain a "you can do it" attitude. Always encourage.

* Personal notes and positive comments from you go a long way in building a positive self-concept.

sex equity

* Watch out for sex-role stereotyping in your own talk. Do you say "the nurse . . . she" and "the lawyer . . . he"? Work to change that habit. Say "the nurse" and "the lawyer." It does not matter if the person is male or female. Refer to "room parent" rather than "room mother," and maybe a father will volunteer for the job.

* Assign the same kinds of chores to boys and girls. Girls can carry books and boys can sweep floors and wash lunch tables. (See jobs.)

* While you might not be able to get rid of a textbook that usually or always portrays women as homemakers, you can point out that this may or may not be the case in the kids' homes. State that women hold responsible jobs both in the home and outside the home, as do men.

* Consider constructing a jobs bulletin board with male and female truck drivers, secretaries, lawyers, nurses, and mechanics. (See **career education**.)

* Try to make yourself aware of the subtle ways in which we foster sex stereotypes.

1. Avoid using words like *men* or *mankind* when you mean "people."

2. Use *he/she* and *her/him,* but be aware that this is awkward to read. Another choice is to use *he* and *she* alternately, *he* in one paragraph and *she* in the next. Our choice is to use *they, them,* and *their.*

3. Instead of *postman,* use *mail carrier.* Say "The mail carrier does . . ." instead of "He does . . ."—the mail carrier may be a woman.

4. Be aware that out of 50 stories in your students' reading book, only 5 might be about women. Supplement these with books about women in leadership roles. Stock your classroom library with such books and ask your school librarian to order books that portray women in leadership roles or in previously male-dominated careers.

5. When you see pictures of men or women in stereotypical occupations, such as the male executive and the female homemaker, point out that males are also homemakers and females are also executives.

6. Watch out for disparaging references, such as "cute secretary" or "male nurse."

7. Watch for descriptions of men that portray them as dominant, nonemotional, aggressive, strong, and competitive and for descriptions of women that portray them as subordinate, emotional, weak, unintelligent, or silly. If the descriptions are generalized to mean all men or all women, point out the fallacy in these kinds of portrayals: Character traits are not peculiar to one sex.

8. Be aware of how men and women are portrayed socially—she as hostess, he as bartender. *She* serves dinner to *his* boss. Jobs should not be defined by sex. Boys can water plants and bake cookies for the class party while girls transport books and set up audio-visual equipment.

specialists

By working closely with specialists, you can better control your class. By befriending the specialists, they will be more likely to call on you and your class if there is something good to be shared.

* If you are not by nature a prompt person, be sure you are prompt with a specialist. When you make a specialist late, you throw off the plans for your class, and your students lose out.

* Don't forget your specialist friends at the beginning and end of the school year, when things are hectic. Classroom teachers have kids to help them with stacking, packing, loading, cleaning, or rearranging. Specialists don't. Lend a kid to a specialist friend; the kid will enjoy it, too.

standards

Go over standards in your mind and make sure they are really important to you. When you are happy with them, present them to your class and stick by them throughout the year. For example:

1. If having a kid's name in the right-hand corner of the paper is important to you because it makes recording grades easier, then state this requirement.

2. In addition to having the kid's name in the right-hand corner, is it important to have it last name first? First *and* last name? If so, require it.

3. Would it help to have the kid include in the paper heading the bell number? Row number? Anything else?

storage

* Keep sets of bulletin board letters in plastic freezer containers. Separate the letters into smaller groups, for example, A-B-C in one container, D-E-F in the next. Label the outside of the container

* Store charts in the order in which you will use them during the year.

* Avoid storing items that are feasts for critters. Sometimes it's hard to know what falls into this category. To our dismay, we learned that food roaches eat green tempera! They practically devoured a lovely chart we had on the layers of the atmosphere.

* In some schools, everything must go home in June. If this is true in your school, take home what you have finished using at the end of each month. That way you will be left with only a few essentials to haul at the end of the year. The same procedure could be used at the beginning of the year, bringing to school only those items you need for the first couple of months.

* Keep a judicious eye on all your materials for frays, dogears, or fading. When a chart or poster is looking a bit shaggy, replace it with a bright, new copy and laminate it so it will last longer.

* If you haven't used something in two years, toss it.

* Consider making your own bookshelves or storage shelves out of 1-by-12-inch pine shelving and cinder blocks. Painted or unpainted, this works fine underneath the windows.

stress

Stress results from an individual's response to events in his or her life. Negative events (the death of a spouse, the loss of a job, a divorce) can produce stress; however, *positive* events (the birth of a baby, a new job, a wedding) can also produce stress. Stress is a reaction to a situation and is not the situation itself. Some reactions to stressful events are positive, healthy, and productive; others are negative, unhealthy, and counterproductive. For example, consider a situation in which a dictatorial principal affects the lives of many people. The amount of stress felt by each person and the method by which each person handles the situation are different: One teacher may react to the dictatorship with griping and complaining, alcohol abuse, and frequent illness; another teacher may take up jogging and find a support group to talk with; a third teacher may transfer to another school; and a fourth teacher may resign from teaching altogether.

* Be aware of the possible stress-producing situations that you may encounter in teaching. Some of them are:

1. loss of job, involuntary transfer, or involuntary reassignment (full-time specialist to half-day specialist and half-day classroom teacher)
2. discipline problems
3. lack of positive reinforcement
4. lack of student achievement
5. poor quality in-services
6. low faculty morale
7. grading
8. poor student attitude
9. not being prepared
10. too many students in your class
11. poor scheduling
12. lesson planning
13. lack of adequate materials
14. threat of malpractice suits
15. extra duty assignments (cafeteria, detention hall, in-school suspension)
16. record keeping and paper work
17. parent–teacher conferences
18. student absences
19. constant interruptions
20. pressure to improve test scores
21. parents' lack of support
22. individualization
23. low pay and no advancement
24. recertification requirements
25. inhibited creativity
26. observations and evaluations
27. receiving new students all through the year
28. underutilization of abilities and skills
29. work overload
30. poor classroom conditions (cold, hot, crowded, shabby)
31. nonparticipation in decisions

✱ Be on the lookout for symptoms of unhealthy management of stress:

tension	workaholism
headaches	loss of appetite
unexplained crying	overeating
backaches	insomnia
irritability	sleeping too much
fatigue	frequent illness
restlessness	frequent accidents
anxiety	alcohol abuse
depression	drug abuse
frustration	increased cigarette
feeling of isolation	smoking
cynicism and griping	unnecessary risk taking
guilt	lack of social interest
indecisiveness	doubts of one's ability or
procrastination	adequacy
boredom	hypersensitivity

✱ The following are suggestions for handling stress in a positive, healthy, and productive way:

1. Get an adequate amount of sleep.
2. Eat right.
3. Get some kind of physical exercise regularly: jogging, tennis, racquetball, walking, swimming, aerobic dancing, calisthenics. It's healthy and makes you feel good because you are accomplishing something.
4. Plan some "me time" daily. Do something you enjoy.
5. Arrive at school early and give yourself an extra few minutes to relax before the bell.
6. Stay after school a while to unwind. Socialize, tie up loose ends, prepare for the next day, or form an exercise group.
7. Know and accept your strengths and weaknesses.
8. Trade off strengths with a co-worker. One of us spells poorly and the other has no facility for math. So, one checks all the written communication and the other does all the figuring.
9. Minimize worry by being well organized and ready for the responsibilities you have assumed.

10. See mistakes as learning experiences rather than as self-defeating experiences.
11. Find someone you can tell it all to, no holds barred. This person should be able to give you honest feedback.
12. Learn to say no. Do not accept more responsibility than you can handle easily.
13. Reduce conflict in personal relationships by being more accepting of others' limitations and opinions.
14. Take a look at your life and analyze your standards. Can you comfortably lower your standards for yourself? Ask yourself what's important to you. For example, if cleaning the house on Saturday is a drudge and leaves no time for family fun, consider the alternatives:
    a. Clean the house during the week at night.
    b. Pay somebody to do it.
    c. Share the jobs with other family members.
    d. Cut your cleaning time in half and live with what remains undone.
15. Associate with positive, enthusiastic people.
16. Avoid such escape routes as drugs and alcohol.
17. Maintain a sense of humor.
18. Don't give up. If necessary, seek outside help.

substitutes

* Know in advance how you are going to get your plans to school if you cannot drag yourself there.

* Always leave plans for more than could possibly be done in a day. Mark some of it "optional" if you prefer, but give the substitute plenty to choose from. Leave extra dittos and fun things for kids to do. Leave the answer sheets for any dittos you prepare.

* Be careful of what you write in plans for substitutes; a substitute could be a parent or a friend of a parent of one of your students. You needn't make remarks like "Keep your eye on Jimmy. He'll drive you crazy." You do not need the hassle it'll cause if the sub is Jimmy's mother's friend and he or she tells Jimmy's mother.

* Make sure to inform the substitute of health problems and about everyone who goes anywhere during the day. A substitute has a need—indeed, a right—to know this.

* Make plans in advance for another teacher to take unruly students from a substitute if necessary; do the same for your colleagues when they are sick.

* Early in the year, find a kid who appears to be dependable. Check this kid out thoroughly by giving him or her administrative duties: lunch count, attendance, picking up library books, alphabetizing papers. Then recommend that student as an aid to the substitute.

* Make a notebook of quick ideas for the substitute and leave the notebook with your plans. We call these "Tricks for the Substitute." Substitutes can use them as time fillers or free-time activities or in place of a cancelled activity. These can be dittos of word searches, easy art projects, math puzzles, or word problems.

* To make a substitute's life easier:

1. Leave detailed lesson plans with special times or places color-coded or underlined.
2. Leave the textbooks that the substitute will need, with bookmarks in place, stacked in the order in which the substitute will use them.
3. Leave dittos, charts, and forms stacked in the order in which they will be used. Label each one as to the time it is to be used and the group it's for.
4. Leave updated seating charts. (See **seating charts**.)
5. Leave detailed lunchroom and dismissal procedures.
6. Encourage the substitute to give you feedback about the day. Leave paper and pencil or a space right on your plans for this. Ask for suggestions of ways you could improve your plans for substitutes.

supplies

Necessary
- colored pens
- pencils
- grease pencils
- markers
- stapler and staples
- large scissors
- ruler
- yard stick
- paper clips
- straight pins
- rubber bands
- note paper and envelopes
- thumbtacks
- construction paper
- glue
- cellophane tape
- masking tape
- dictionary
- tissues
- watch

Nice to Have
- pins
- typewriter
- hammer and nails
- screwdriver and screws
- plastic pin-back letters
- stencils for letters
- sliding grade chart
- index cards
- folders
- colored chalk
- staple remover
- string
- colored tape
- yarn
- chart clips
- magnets
- pencil holders
- stamps
- puzzles
- games

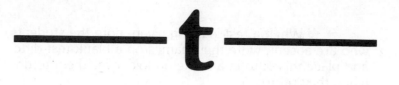

tests and quizzes

* When preparing tests, use a number of questions that is easily divisible into 100. For example, use 25 questions worth 4 points each or 20 questions worth 5 points each. This will save you time when grading.

* If you construct a matching, true/false, or fill-in-the-blank test, arrange the answers in a pattern you can easily memorize for grading purposes. For instance, TFTFF—TFTFF—TFTFF are grouped in fives for easy memorization. When using letters, come up with words or sentences that are easy to memorize. Change your pattern often, and don't be too obvious.

* Put the objective of the test at the top of the test. This is a good reference for conferences.

* Don't test on days when you know students will be out—for example, the day after the senior prom or the day before a major holiday.

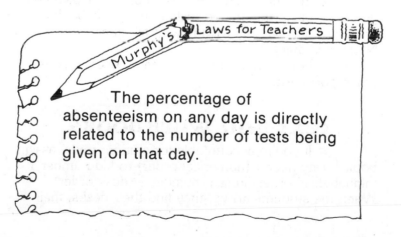

Murphy's Laws for Teachers

The percentage of absenteeism on any day is directly related to the number of tests being given on that day.

* When a test is being given, note the students who are absent, write their names on a blank test ditto and place this ditto in a make-up folder for them to do when they return.

* When students have handed in their tests, arrange them in alphabetical or numerical order for easy recording of their grades.

* When you are grading, if the normal curve doesn't come out, check your teaching, unusual circumstances on the day the test was given (was there snow or a fire drill?), or the fairness of the test.

* Make positive comments on test papers. Try to help the kids rather than put them down. The little stamp that says "poor work" is not the way to help kids improve their work or their self-esteem. It would be better to tell them what they can do to improve.

* When you are returning a graded test to your students, have them check for the errors in your correction, correct their own errors, have the test signed by a parent, and return it to you for filing. Use these tests at conference time.

* Readily admit to mistakes in grading and change the grade. Do not defend a mistake. Give back tests and review papers openly. Ask for questions about tests or grades, because it is easier to deal with kids than to deal with the parents and the principal. Teachers *do* make mistakes.

* Encourage students to record their own test grades or paste the graded tests in their notebooks so they and their parents will know at all times "how Norman is doing."

* For related topics see **conferences, grades,** and **report cards.**

text and workbooks

* If you're accountable for student texts, assign book set number 1 (numerical order) to kid number 1 (alphabetical order) in seat number 1 (desk order). When the students arrive, they find their desks, their

A System for Accounting for and Distributing Textbooks

name tags, and their books. This is the ultimate in organization. (If books are not already numbered, use a smearproof, waterproof pen to mark the number at the top of the spine of the book.) For easy checking at inventory time, have the students stack on a counter all the books of a set in numerical order. For example, all math books are stacked and #21 is missing. With a blink of an eye, you can tell which book is missing, and whose it is.

In addition, this book-accounting system shows the students that you are ready for them and in control; saves valuable teaching time because you can start right away; keeps students busy looking at their new books while you tend to other things; seats students alphabetically, which may prevent discipline problems by separating best friends, and tends to help new kids assimilate more easily.

* Keep a record of the conditions of the books so that at the end of the year you won't mistakenly accuse a student of misusing a book. Having students sign for the books in their present conditions tends to make them more responsible for the books.

* Explain your standards for the care of rented or free textbooks on the first day. Instruct all students to cover their books immediately. Many businesses offer free book covers, but a brown paper grocery bag makes a good, sturdy cover that will last about a year. Students can also purchase clear plastic book covers which are advertised like panty hose—one size fits all!

* Tell students the penalties for lost or destroyed books. Will they receive final reports if their books are lost? Will their transcripts be sent? Will they graduate?

* Tell students the cost of replacing a book that is lost or mutilated, and suggest that they earn the money for a replacement.

* Encourage the use of bookmarks.

* Don't lend one student's books to another student; discourage borrowing and lending of books altogether.

* Workbooks show signs of wear early in the year. Use wide masking tape on the spines and inside the front and back covers to give them a longer life.

* For related topics see **beginning the year, behavior problems, control, discipline,** and **school property.**

time management

* Plan for a week, a month, or even a year at a time. Run all dittos, prepare all transparencies, and assemble all papers or charts needed. Do as much of this as you can at one time. Once your mind is set for one activity—running dittos, ordering films—stick with that activity until it is done. You will save yourself time by handling things once.

* Handle papers only one time and, if at all possible, answer whatever it is right on the paper you receive.

* Rather than have the students move about in the class, *you* move. For reading groups or math groups, pull your chair up to them rather than have eight of them screeching chairs to gather around you.

The only time you are a few minutes late all year is the time the supervisor will be waiting in your room for you . . . looking at the clock.

* Use the overhead projector so the lesson can be written before class and saved. Writing on the overhead is also easier for you than writing on the board. If you teach the same subject several times a day, think of the time you can save by writing on the overhead projector.

* A schedule on the board saves questions and time when you move from subject to subject.

* Use your 3 x 5 cards for ideas and notes to yourself. Keep them on your person at all times. (See ideas.)

* Never waste a minute; always carry something to do. If you go to use the office phone and the line is busy, use that five minutes to complete some bitty task you brought with you. For that matter, never be without something to do outside of school, too. While you are waiting in a doctor's office, you could sketch a bulletin board you've planned.

* Have your lesson plans in order so you don't have to flounder for something to do. Plan just a bit more than you need if you are in doubt.

* Make a To Do list each day before you leave school. Then go home and relax. Next morning when you arrive, check your To Do list and your Daily Reminder File (see daily reminder file), and you are on your way. On your To Do list, do the thing that is the yuckiest first. After that, the others will seem easy.

✶ Even though you will simultaneously answer a question about last night's television programming, listen to a student's problem with her sister, and respond to the secretary on the speaker about a new student you will be receiving, try to concentrate on one thing at a time.

✶ Set deadlines, write them down, and post them where you can see them.

✶ Anything students can capably do for you, let them do. Students can file dittos, alphabetize papers, wash chalkboards, run projectors, and pass out and collect materials.

✶ Have a place for everything so you don't waste time looking for things.

✶ Color-coordinate everything pertaining to one subject. If 6th-grade English books are yellow, store your dittos for 6th-grade English in yellow construction-paper folders, and highlight the plans for 6th-grade English in yellow in your plan book. Keep your notes for 6th-grade English in a yellow notebook and encourage your students to do the same. Your eye will waste no time in helping you gather all the stuff you need for 6th-grade English.

✶ Most textbooks are kept by school systems for five or more years. Spend the extra time the first year outlining chapters, making charts, taking notes, preparing dittos and transparencies, designing bulletin boards, listing films and filmstrips that correlate with the text, and planning for special activities. Once this is done, you have your work cut out for you for the next few years. You need only to delete or add ideas.

✶ If you must choose, put your extra efforts into the text that has just been adopted, not the one that is four years old.

✶ Make a movable or erasable seating chart. (See seating charts.)

✶ Determine your most productive time of the day and do your work then. If you do your best work early in the morning, try to get to school a little earlier Then you can lizard around in the lounge in the afternoon because your work is done.

traffic flow in the classroom

* During the first week of school, keep your eyes open for trouble spots caused by poor desk arrangement. Fix all possible trouble areas (areas where students congregate: pencil sharpener, water fountain, sink, your desk, learning centers) so that the least congestion is caused and the fewest students are bothered.

* To reduce movement in the classroom, ask that students have something ready to do at their desks when they have completed their work. This assures the other students the quiet they need to finish their work. Students may be permitted to read books or play quiet games so long as they are seated. A schedule of assignments on the board may encourage some students to start on the next assignment.

* Whenever possible, move yourself, not the kids.

* Give comprehensive directions to cut down on traffic in the classroom. If your schedule reads spelling–lunch–math, at the end of your spelling period, tell the class to put away their spelling books, get their lunches, and have their math materials ready for their return from lunch.

* Have a system for distributing and collecting materials. For example, collect all completed assignments at one time to keep individuals from wandering up to your desk. Reduced movement in the classroom reduces confusion, noise, and distractions to working students.

transportation

* Post bus numbers, loads or shifts, names of walkers to and from school, and any other information pertaining to transportation. Check this information the first day as soon as the students have arrived and settled down. This is important—you do not want the responsibility of driving 13 kids home on the first day of school because they missed the bus.

* Know that you are liable for the safety of any student you transport in your vehicle. Our advice is *don't.*

* Demand a note if there is any change in the child's routine transportation. If Meghan is supposed to go home with Greta for a Scouts meeting, demand a note. If Peter and Tim must switch to bus 163 to go to the sitter's, demand a note.

* Do not leave the school grounds with one of your kids left unsupervised waiting for a parent.

* Avoid field trips that will require paid transportation if it will burden parents of kids in the classroom.

* For a related topic see **field trips.**

tutoring

* Tutoring can be lucrative, especially in the summer months. Most school systems have specific guidelines concerning tutoring. Know the guidelines before you accept a tutoring job.

* Some school systems or individual schools have lists of available tutors. If yours doesn't, suggest compiling a list of willing tutors. Your name could be the first on the list!

u

umpire

There will be fewer arguments and better feelings if you umpire competitive games. Make sure you know the rules for the game, then make your calls with authority. Playing games with your class can be a treat for them and you. It can also be a stress reducer.

unavoidable mistakes

We all make mistakes, and it is a waste of one's time to try to be perfect. Do your absolute best, and try not to make the same mistakes over and over again. Learn from your mistakes, but don't berate yourself unnecessarily over them. Admit your mistakes, apologize if you have caused someone needless trouble or worry, and then get on with it.

V

vacation

✱ Begin your work on an advanced degree. It is easier to schedule time to write papers, do the required reading, and attend classes when you don't have the added responsibility of your own students. For a change of scenery, attend an out-of-state college.

✱ Sign up for an educational tour for credit. Tours all over the world are offered through universities, professional organizations, and professional magazines. Many of these tours are for college credit, both undergraduate and graduate.

✱ Attend the workshops, conventions, and conferences you are not able to attend in the winter because of a jam-packed schedule.

✱ Look for a summer job that is totally out of your field—office work, life guarding, department store help, outside sales. Some of these jobs made us really want to come back in September.

✱ Consider constructing all your bulletin boards for next year. Have everything drawn, colored, laminated, and cut out ready to go.

✱ Do something creative that you have never done before: Write a book, paint, take piano or ballet lessons, hook a rug, refinish furniture.

✱ If you like, do nothing but read, watch the soaps, sleep late, and play. You deserve it.

vase

Keep an inexpensive vase for flowers you may receive during the year. Who knows? The superintendent may just send flowers to you for the outstanding job you are doing! *Psst!* If the super doesn't, send them to yourself with a nice note!

violence

You know that violence is not permitted between students, but did you know that violence is not permitted between teacher and student? Your insurance will not cover it unless you are defending yourself.

* If you sense violence toward you rising in a student, diffuse it first. Don't let it get out of hand.

1. Don't threaten the student.
2. Don't touch the student.
3. Don't back the student into a corner.
4. Lower your voice.
5. Don't show fear if you feel it.

* When two students are slinging punches and you are tempted to step in and separate them, STOP! Survey the situation and decide how safe it is for you to step in between them.
* Work on personal rights and values as part of your social studies lessons. Set up hypothetical situations and open-ended discussions for guiding your students to nonviolent behavior.
* For related topics see behavior problems and discipline.

vision

(See health: physical and mental.)

visual materials

(See audio-visual aids.)

voice

For a real eye-opener, tape your own voice to see what the students have to listen to all day. Check your volume, pacing, diction, pitch, modulation, and elocution. Be sure to check for your tweeters and woofers. Are they acceptable? If not, work on them so the kids in the back row can hear and understand you.

volunteers and aides

* If you have been assigned an aide or a volunteer to work with you in your room, make the best use of the aide's time. Have the aide:

1. supervise seatwork, games, and learning centers
2. assist students with projects
3. work with special students
4. escort groups to the library for specific work
5. distribute and collect students' materials
6. gather and set up A-V equipment and materials
7. grade objective tests
8. record grades or test results
9. make ditto masters and run off sets of dittos
10. inventory classroom materials
11. introduce new students to the school
12. collect and record money for trips
13. construct bulletin boards
14. supervise the classroom in an emergency
15. supervise one group while you are nearby with another

voting

Conduct voting for important positions, such as SCA president, class president or room representative, by *closed* ballot. It is crushing to Bob to find that his own vote was the only one he received.

W

watch

Invest in a reliable watch with a second hand. You are probably the only person in nine states whose lunch period begins at 12:02 and ends at precisely 12:32. There are a dozen things you'll need the second hand for, including timing tests and tuning in to the educational television program that begins at exactly 10:33:5.

weather

* Child neglect is considered child abuse. Check on kids who routinely come to school improperly dressed. Notify the proper authority in your school. (See child abuse.)

* Keep a sweater in your room for either a needy kid or yourself if the weather changes or the heat goes off. (It may never have come on!)

* Have an alternate plan for PE period in case the weather changes. If you have planned to play volleyball outdoors and it is raining, have an indoor game ready.

worksheets

* Put the objective at the top of all worksheets and call your students' attention to it.

* If you leave a set of worksheets with a substitute, be sure you leave an answer sheet. The substitute may want to check them for you or may be asked questions by the class.

* Put the names of the absent kids on worksheets and file them in a make-up folder for them to do when they return.

* If it is not absolutely necessary for students to write on a dittoed worksheet, let them mark answers on a sheet of their own paper. Collect the unused worksheets and save them for another group.

* While all worksheets are not of earth-shattering importance, students like to know how they do. Make the answers available to the class either through discussion, by grading, or by having a kid put the answers on the board.

x-rated language

Don't use it, and don't let the kids use it, either. In your case, if you slip, it is merely a moment before the news reaches the office, and this can open a can of worms. Use your judgment. If you choose to let fly with a string of beauties before your class of 11th-graders because you think they'll identify with you and your language, prepare yourself for the consequences.

y

yardstick

Purchase one with standard measure on one side and metric measure on the other. Also tell the students to have metric rulers on hand. Most math and science books we've reviewed deal with metric measure, so this is a safe purchase for you and the kids. Patronize a merchant who gives away yardsticks or (oops!) metersticks.

yawn

If you see one in class, there'll soon be dozens—yours included. Before that happens:

1. Open a few windows or the door.
2. Have the class stand, and lead them in stretches or exercises for a few minutes.
3. Change the pace of the lesson to a more active one.
4. Take a water break.
5. If the class is still yawning, take a good look at the lesson. Beef it up and make it less deadly!

yelling

✶ Don't. It's rough on the vocal cords and wears you down.
✶ For related topics see **behavior problems, control, discipline,** and **voice.**

Z

zeal

Enthusiasm is contagious. Put on a good display. The students pick up on your zeal and know when it is lacking. (See stress.)

zero

Be aware of the impact a big red zero at the top of a paper has on a student. Is that what you want to achieve? Approaching problems from a positive standpoint usually gets better results than approaching them from a negative standpoint does. (See grades.)

zipper

Don't let students (or teachers) go around all day with a zipper down, a slip showing, or spinach between their teeth. Be a pal and discreetly make them aware of the problem.

zombie

Better known as Teacher on a Friday Afternoon. Also what you may feel like after a trip to the zoo.

zzz's

What we hope did not happen to you as you read this book!

about the authors

Ann Salisbury Harrison received a B.S. in education from Rhode Island College in Providence, Rhode Island. She received an M.S. in guidance and counseling from Old Dominion University, Norfolk, Virginia and is now in advanced studies in Educational Administration at Old Dominion. Ms. Harrison has taught fifth grade for twelve years and is now a secondary school guidance counselor in Virginia Beach, Virginia. She has authored reports, school-wide self-studies, curriculum guides, and in-service plans for the school system.

Frances Burton Spuler holds a B.A. in English and an M.S. in Educational Administration from Old Dominion University, Norfolk, Virginia. She has taught fourteen years in grades two through adult education and is currently teaching in grade six. She has authored reports, in-service plans for the school system, curriculum guides, and school-wide self-studies.